BE HEALED

by
Marilyn Hickey

Marilyn Hickey Ministries
P.O. Box 17340 • Denver, Colorado 80217

BE HEALED

ISBN 1-56441-021-8

Unless otherwise indicated,
all Scripture quotations
are taken from the
King James Version of the Bible.

FOREWORD

Marilyn Hickey is a precious gift to the Body of Christ who possesses a wealth of knowledge and insight of God's Word.

I have known Marilyn personally for 19 years—since the early days of my ministry—and I can confidently say her ministry possesses both integrity and purity.

In my opinion, she is one of the world's leading Bible teachers. She is a gifted and anointed Bible expositor who blesses her audience with a rich understanding of deep Biblical truth. The lives of people who attend her meetings are profoundly impacted for the kingdom of God.

When Marilyn spoke to me about her interest in writing a book on healing, I immediately felt a witness in my spirit that this book needed to be written. I know the results will be a blessing to multitudes since there is not enough sound material written on the healing ministry.

It is a pleasure for me to recommend this book. I believe it will be a blessing to all whose lives will be touched by reading BE HEALED.

Benny Hinn, Pastor
Orlando Christian Center

CONTENTS

Chapter One

GOD WANTS YOU WELL!

"In Jesus' name, **Be Healed**!" Power, like a million volts of electricity, issued from those words! Instantly the woman felt God's touch on her body, and she knew she was being healed. She actually felt the large fibroid tumor which had invaded her body begin to shrink; she could even watch her body regain its normal shape.

Only a miracle had kept the woman alive for nearly five years. The tumor had been gradually snuffing out her life. Wrapping itself around the internal organs of her body, it had pushed out her stomach and shoved the lower abdominal organs upward against her heart and lungs. The woman had felt the tumor inching its way toward her heart. Nevertheless, her spiritual "heart" remained fixed in God, and every day she lived, she lived expecting a miracle. "I will not die, but live and declare the works of the LORD" she repeatedly reminded herself as she quoted Psalms 118:17!

The woman's condition had been diagnosed and confirmed by several doctors. Although they knew what was happening, none of them dared operate because it was more risky to attempt a removal of the tumor than it was to leave the tumor alone. It was a "no win" situation. Gradually her life was ebbing away. The tumor was bad enough, but the hemorrhaging caused by the tumor was even more threatening. Blood transfusions would have been beneficial, but the doctors were hesitant because of the threat of AIDS. In spite of her condition, the woman had never given up. At the moment of her healing, she was among a group who had gone with me on a short term mission trip to China.

Somewhere high above the Pacific Ocean, as the big jetliner soared through the skies toward home, *the miracle* happened! God had spoken to another woman in the group and said, "This thing will not kill your friend; I'm going to deliver her now, as you speak the word of healing." Then the precious Holy Spirit gave her a glimpse inside the afflicted body of her new friend. With her spiritual eyes the astonished woman saw something that looked like a tree whose roots were in the woman's uterine area, then the "tree" branched out wrapping itself around all the other organs, and even then was reaching for her heart.

As the one woman prayed for the other, the power of God enveloped them both and surged into the body of the sick woman. She literally felt the tumor shrinking from around her heart, then her lungs and stomach. After her other organs were released from the tentacles of the tumor, the Lord began putting all her organs back in place. In a matter of moments, God had done what no physician had been able to do in years. The woman was healed by the touch of the **Great Physician**! Documented records prove the woman's dramatic healing. She is well today and rejoicing in the Lord.

How thrilling! I get excited every time I see or hear a miracle of healing. The Lord is continually showing Himself to be the same today as He has ever been. Let me tell you, God is "up to date." What He is doing in our day is as current as the headlines in this morning's paper. You don't have to read about His mighty works in the Bible to know that He is your healer. Whoever you are, wherever you are, you can experience His healing touch this very moment! Over and over again, the Lord is proving that He wants to heal you and make you whole.

THE PURSUIT OF HEALING

There have always been two kinds of people in the world, either those who are well or those who are sick—and the sick are doing everything they can to get well. If you are ill, my heart's desire is that the information you receive within the pages of this book may stir your faith and produce your healing. If you are enjoying good health, learn how to stay that way. If you picked up this book because you have a friend or loved one who is ill, I'm believing you'll learn to pray for that person with faith and confidence **and see results**. If you are not convinced that God is your healer, I believe the Word of God will change your thinking. Whatever your reason for reading this book, I hope it will expand your knowledge and change you in a very positive way. Here's to **GOOD HEALTH**!

Few topics catch our interest and attention more than health and healing. Much of our time and money is spent pursuing good health. Medicine has become so specialized that we need a different doctor for every problem or body part. Large hospitals and medical centers etch the skyline of every major city and even the smallest towns boast of a clinic. "State-of-the-art" equipment is able to probe and image the most remote and inaccessible regions of our bodies. Let's face it, medicine has become a trillion-dollar industry; and the cost of staying well is staggering.

Preventive medicine has come to the forefront in recent years. After all, don't we prefer to stay well rather than need to be healed? We now have physicians who practice only in the area of nutrition and prevention, and holistic medicine has become a byword. Shopping malls have nutrition stores with shelves stocked with every imaginable vitamin, herb, drink, etc., intended to promote health. People watch their cholesterol and triglycerides like a financier would watch the latest Dow Jones Average. Most of us are running (or walking) after a healthier body. Fitness programs and fitness machines, not to mention health clubs, are all the rage. Has our all-consuming interest in good health become a new "religion" in our day?

In spite of all this, there are still multitudes of people who are ill. I appreciate what medical science is doing to improve our health, and I am thankful for every doctor practicing his skills to provide healing for our bodies. However, we know there are things they cannot do; and you may be one of those who is stricken with an incurable disease. Let me tell you that nothing is too hard for God. There is just no touch like the touch of Jesus!

The unusual healing of the woman I mentioned earlier reminds me of a woman Jesus healed while He was here on earth. That woman had been hemorrhaging for 12 years, had spent all the money she had on doctors, and instead of getting better, she was getting worse. It took a lot of courage to approach Jesus, but what she had heard about Jesus's healing power convinced her that if she could even touch His clothes she would be healed. Her faith was instantly rewarded, and Jesus commended her faith by saying, "Go in peace, your faith has made you whole." (See Luke 8:43-48.) You see, nothing takes the Lord by surprise; everything He has done in the past, He can do today for you.

Several facts catch my attention in the miraculous healing of this woman. Even in a large crowd, Jesus had time for *one* "insignificant" woman who touched Him *by faith*. Jesus knew the woman could slip away undetected, and she would go with a whole body. However, Jesus cared so much for the woman that He stopped her and gave her His **Word** on the matter, " . . . *thy faith hath made thee whole; go in peace."* He had the power, and she had the faith. What a combination!

When we talk about healing, we almost always think of physical healing; but God's healing is for the *whole* person. Under the inspiration of the Holy Spirit, the apostle Paul prayed: *"And the very God of peace sanctify you wholly; and I pray God your whole spirit and soul and body be preserved blameless unto the coming of our Lord Jesus Christ"* (I Thessalonians 5:23). God wants all of you well. His Word declares that healing is for your entire being: your spirit, your soul, and your body.

Notice with me that Paul put the spirit first. Without spirit wholeness, neither your soul nor your body can truly stay in good health. Spirit wholeness means having the eternal life of God in your spirit by asking Jesus to be your Savior. Spirit "wellness" is maintained by a continual feeding on God's Word. Just as your body needs **whole**some food to maintain good health, so your spirit needs the wholesome Word of God to maintain good health. You certainly need a strong healthy spirit to be an overcomer in life.

The Lord also wants you well in your soul. Your soul is made up of your mind, your emotions, and also your will. The will is the course-setter and direction-finder of every individual. Being mentally and emotionally able to make right choices and right decisions is a very important factor in wholeness. Lives can be ruined through bad choices, can't they? Look what happened to all of us when Adam and Eve ate the forbidden fruit. Now that was a bad choice!

Soul "sickness" is often the result of choosing to hold onto anger or bitterness without forgiving others—or one's self;

guilt is a terrible tormentor. It might come through a decision to commit adultery, thereby breaking up a home and bringing overwhelming sorrow and depression; or it might be an error in judgment which brought business failure. Whatever the case, we now have doctors and therapists for the soul-sick. Isn't it wonderful to know it is God's will for us to be mentally and emotionally healthy, and that God, the Holy Spirit, can give to us the wisdom to make right and profitable decisions!

Not long ago the doors of a Texas cafeteria swung open and a barrage of bullets ended the lives of over 20 innocent people. A man had entered the eating establishment and "gunned down" people he'd never seen before. Another recent headline horrified us all with the news of a man so disturbed that he murdered 15 people, dismembered their bodies, then proceeded to eat the body parts! Our modern society is flooded with individuals who aren't mentally or emotionally whole. You and I live in a sin-sick world, and only Jesus can make the difference.

Let me share some "good news" that you won't read in the newspaper. A Christian couple went to prison authorities and obtained permission to meet with a female serial killer. This hardened criminal gave her life to Christ and was filled with the Holy Spirit when the couple shared God's love. The man and woman, themselves filled with divine love, have legally adopted this convicted murderess. Whatever punishment the woman must suffer for her crimes, she knows that *old things have passed away and that all things have become new* in Christ Jesus. (See II Corinthians 5:17.) What a miraculous healing!

Wherever you are and whatever your circumstance, *the Lord wants you whole.* If you have a broken heart, He wants to heal it. If you have a broken pocketbook, He wants to heal it. If you have a sick, infirm, or broken body, the Lord wants to heal it. *Wholeness* is the will of God for every individual, and certainly nothing is too difficult for the One Who created the universe and fashioned your physical body. The Lord is able to heal your circumstances and your relationships just as easily as He can heal your body—if you ask and believe:

And this is the confidence that we have in him, that, if we ask any thing according to his will, he heareth us: And if we know that he hear us, whatsoever we ask, we know that we have the petitions that we desired of him (I John 5:14,15). *Beloved, I wish above all things that thou mayest prosper and be in health, even as thy soul prospereth* (III John 2).

MADE IN THE IMAGE OF GOD

When God designed the first man and woman, they were absolutely perfect. The master plan was set in motion by the Father Who said, *"Let **us** make man in **our** image."* Then Jesus executed the plan by scooping up a lump of clay and shaping a man; out of man He fashioned a woman. When speaking of Jesus, Colossians 1:16 tells us that "... *all things ... were created by him, and for him."* In John 1:3 we read that by God's Word were all things made, "... *and without Him nothing was made that was made."* Verse 14 of John 1 positively identifies the Word as Jesus Christ; but not until the Holy Spirit breathed the life of God into Adam's spirit did Adam become a living being. All three persons of the Trinity were involved.

13

So you see, you have been made in the likeness and image of the Father, the Son, and the Holy Spirit. You and I are just "chips off the old block." When God made you in His image—spirit, soul, and body—He was just as interested in your body as in any other part of your being. He is the same yesterday, today, and forever. When God made our human father and mother, He was so pleased with His workmanship that He stood back, looked at them, and said, "Just what we wanted. This is very good."

Ecclesiastes 3:14 states, *"I know that, whatsoever God doeth, it shall be for ever: nothing can be put to it, nor any thing taken from it: and God doeth it, that men should fear before him."* When God made man, He made him very complete, very good, and very wonderful. Even scientists who are agnostics or atheists all agree with the psalmist David who said, *"I am fearfully and wonderfully made."* These people can't even begin to understand the intricacies and the beauty of the body. It is beyond them. Why? Because it is made by God, made to be like Him! I want to tell you that your body is a gift from God:

> *For thou hast possessed my reins: thou hast covered me in my mother's womb. I will praise thee; for I am fearfully and wonderfully made: marvellous are thy works; and that my soul knoweth right well. My substance was not hid from thee, when I was made in secret, and curiously wrought . . . Thine eyes did see my substance, yet being unperfect; and in thy book all my members were written, which in continuance were fashioned, when as yet there was none of them. How precious also are thy thoughts unto me, O God! how great is the sum of them!* (Psalms 139:13-17).

A TRAITOR IN THE CAMP

Then what on earth happened to the human family? If God made us in His image and likeness, when did sin and sickness enter the picture? Since we know that God is good and everything He created is good, how did Satan and evil come into existence? For the right answers we must look into the Scripture. First we find Satan in Heaven. God created him as the archangel Lucifer in whom was invested the sum of all God's wisdom! This angel was extremely beautiful and gifted in every way. He had great musical ability and probably led all heaven in praises to God. Lucifer was also the anointed cherub who covered the altar of God and was perhaps the greatest of all God's created beings. *But* Lucifer turned his eyes on himself instead of on God; and, instead of being grateful, he became resentful. You may read this account in Isaiah 14:12-15 and Ezekiel 28:12-19.

When Lucifer should have been praising God for his beauty, talent, and position, he became lifted up in pride and set himself *up* for quite a *let down*! At the moment self became the center of attention rather than God, *sin was born* with all its evil consequences. Lucifer decided he would lift his throne above God's throne and enlisted a third part of the angels who rebelled with him. Of course, sin could not exist in the presence of God; so Lucifer and the rebel angels were cast out of God's heaven. God's "Son of the Morning" with all his beauty and ability became darkness, ugliness, and evil. Thus an intense hatred toward God flamed in the heart of the one who became Satan, that old serpent the devil.

But how did the devil set up shop on earth and get into the sickness business? How did he manage to make God's children sick in the first place? Well, the devil got into the sickness business when mankind got into the sin business. God's first family gave the devil just the opportunity for which he looked when those two people succumbed to satanic temptation. Adam and Eve opened the door to sin, and sin opened the door to all Satan's work; sickness and sin are Siamese twins. Tell me, was there any sickness or disease in the garden of Eden? No, because there wasn't any death or dying; and sickness is just progressive death.

Adam and Eve opened a veritable "Pandora's box" when they opened their hearts to sin. They forfeited the earth to Satan who became the "spoiler" of God's perfect creation. Paradise was lost and so was life and fellowship with God. Instead of continuing to have God's nature, Adam and Eve received the devil's nature; a nature filled with sin, sickness, poverty, and death. What sort of nature were Adam and Eve going to pass on to their offspring? Of course, a *sin nature*. Satan had managed to poison the mainstream of humanity with all his evil baggage.

Since Satan is the exact opposite of all God's goodness, his touch brings sickness, disease, and pain. The woman with the issue of blood was touched by the devil before she was touched by the Lord. Notice that when Jesus spoke to the woman He told her to go in peace. He could have said, "Be at ease," and it would have meant the same thing. God's health and blessing brings peace; it puts us at ease. So what does Satan do? He brings dis-ease. Do you realize that when your body is diseased you are out of the peace God intends for you?

> *The thief cometh not, but for to steal, and to kill, and to destroy: I* [Jesus] *am come that they might have life, and that they might have it more abundantly* (John 10:10).

16

When Adam and Eve *obeyed* the devil, they *disobeyed* God and relinquished their God-given authority over the earth to a supernatural being who was more powerful than they were—*without God*. Do you see what Satan purposed? He had flown in the face of God and won. The Lord had made Adam to be god over everything in the earth, but Satan usurped Adam's position and now all that belonged to Adam was Satan's. Therefore, every earthly thing fell with Adam and Eve. It fell into the hands of the deceiver:

Know ye not, that to whom ye yield yourselves servants to obey, his servants ye are to whom ye obey; whether of sin unto death, or of obedience unto righteousness? (Romans 6:16).

Satan isn't just *your* enemy, he is *God's* enemy. He hates you because he hates God and everything that is like God. When the enemy comes with sickness, it is to harm what God has made in His likeness. The devil wants to destroy everything that God loves and for which He cares; he wants to spoil God's image on the earth. Satan's way of getting back at God is to come against you. Does Satan hate your body? Of course he does. Without a healthy body, you cannot live in the fullness God desires; and **without** your body, you can no longer live on this earth to rejoice in the Lord and bring glory to His Name.

Satan knows that every time he hurts you, he hurts the heart of God because God loves you so much. Every parent on earth, who knows the agony of seeing their children sick, has some idea of how God, our heavenly parent, must feel when we are dis-eased. Most parents would willingly take the illness of their children upon themselves rather than have their offspring ill. This is exactly what the Father did for us when Jesus went to the Cross and died for the sickness of sin. The substitutionary death of Jesus, Who was God in the flesh, redeemed us from sin; and in that full redemption was the healing of *your* body!

JESUS PAID THE PRICE

There is no reason for any of us to be confused about who puts sickness on us. Jesus took our sickness and disease upon Himself at Calvary. The Lord paid a price for your wholeness that cannot be measured; Jesus redeemed you from the curse of the law by becoming a curse for you. (See Galatians 3:13.) There is certainly no reason why God would put sickness on His children when He paid such a price to remove it. Would loving parents put sickness on their children to teach them a lesson or to make them love the parents more? That is utter nonsense!

> *Surely He has borne our griefs—sickness, weakness and distress—and carried our sorrows and pain . . . Yet we ignorantly considered Him stricken, smitten and afflicted by God . . . But He was wounded for our transgressions, He was bruised for our guilt and iniquities; the chastisement needful to obtain peace and well-being for us was upon Him, and with the stripes that wounded Him we are healed and made whole* (Isaiah 53:4,5 TAB).

> *Who his own self bare our sins in his own body on the tree, that we, being dead to sins, should live unto righteousness: by whose stripes ye were healed* (I Peter 2:24).

There are many people who think God chastens His children by putting sickness on them. But that idea is not

Biblically sound. Oh yes, all sorts of folks have all sorts of testimonies about how God brought them back to Himself or taught them many lessons needed to be learned during a period of illness. You may have one of those testimonies, and I don't doubt that for a moment. God is a divine opportunist, and He is in the business of turning into good those things intended for evil. Undoubtedly, many people reach out to the Lord when they are sick and distressed; but God doesn't have to make you sick to get your attention. Sickness is from the devil:

> *How God anointed Jesus of Nazareth with the Holy Ghost and with power: who went about doing good, and* **healing all** *that were* **oppressed of the devil;** *for God was with him* (Acts 10:38).
> . . . *For this purpose the Son of God was manifested, that he might destroy the works of the devil* (I John 3:8).

Jesus was anointed with power to heal those oppressed of the devil; He was brought into the world to destroy the devil's work. Is sickness the oppression of the devil; is it his work? If it is, then the sick need to be healed! Look with me at another portion of scripture. Luke 13:10-17 describes a woman who had a *spirit* of infirmity. For eighteen years this infirm spirit had caused the woman's body to be bowed so severely that she could not stand straight. One day when Jesus was teaching in a synagogue He saw this crippled woman in the congregation.

The Lord asked the woman to come to Him and, laying His hands on her, said, *"Woman, thou art loosed from thine infirmity."* Immediately the woman's body straightened, and she gave glory to God. When the religious hypocrites protested, Jesus said, *"And ought not this woman, being a daughter of Abraham,* **whom Satan hath bound,** *lo, these eighteen years, be loosed from this bond on the sabbath day?"* When Jesus said this, "*. . . all his adversaries were ashamed: and all the people rejoiced for all the glorious things that were done by him."*

I am always so delighted when a modern day miracle of healing brings the Scriptures "alive." I want to share just such a remarkable healing told to me by a healing evangelist. In one of his meetings, there was a woman who couldn't be overlooked. She was a pitiful sight! From the waist up her body was completely bent over to one side. She was contorted into a "U" shape and could neither straighten her body nor look up at anything. When the evangelist prayed for her, those nearby heard loud cracking and popping noises and to the amazement of everyone, this woman straightened to an erect position before their eyes. Hallelujah! What a miracle.

THE SIN PRINCIPLE

That poor woman I just described was carrying around in her body the marks of Satan's curse until Jesus touched her and made her whole. Jesus said the curse came from Satan. It did not come from God! Oh yes, the Lord did come back to the garden in Eden, found those whom He had made so lovingly in His image and likeness, and **explained** what the curse would bring to them, to the earth, and to all the creatures of the earth. Remember that all the earth fell with humanity's fall. So the whole earth was "out of kilter"; it was all cursed. There was now a sin principle, a law of sin, working in mankind and in all his environment. Everything was going to obey that law without God's intervention:

For the earnest expectation of the creature waiteth
for the manifestation of the sons of God. For the
creature was made subject to vanity, not
willingly, but by reason of him who hath subjected
the same in hope, Because the creature itself also
shall be delivered from the bondage of corruption
into the glorious liberty of the children of God.
For we know that the whole creation groaneth
and travaileth in pain together until now
(Romans 8:19-22).

Both Adam and Eve immediately exposed their sin nature even though they tried to hide it. Adam blamed God, and he also blamed Eve for his predicament. Eve turned around and blamed the serpent. In the next generation the inherited sin nature was soon exposed when Cain killed his brother because of pride and jealousy. Genesis 3:16-19 generalizes the curse, but Deuteronomy 28:15-68 details the curse which comes from the law of sin and death. Deuteronomy ascribes every manner of sickness to the curse. There is no doubt that sin brings sickness, disease, and everything that is "unwhole." (See I Thessalonians 5:23.)

Now I want your full attention. I am **not** saying that you have committed sin every time you get sick. There are people who put a guilt trip on those who are ill by implying that their sickness is the result of some sin in their life. Remember that the sin principle which brought sickness and death is at work in the earth. Even babies are born with disease, deformity, or some physical or mental handicap, and those precious children have not had the opportunity to sin. Jesus, Himself, made it clear that it is not necessarily sin in an individual that causes their illness:

*And as Jesus passed by, he saw a man which was
blind from his birth. And his disciples asked him,
saying, Master, who did sin, this man, or his
parents, that he was born blind? Jesus answered,
Neither hath this man sinned, nor his parents . . .*
(John 9:1-3).

After telling His followers that it was neither the man nor
his parents who had sinned, Jesus declared that the works
of God should be made manifest in the man. The works of
Satan had produced blindness, but God's work would bring
healing and sight to the man. *"I must work the works of
him that sent me,"* Jesus said; and then He proceeded to
demonstrate that work. Bending over, the Lord spit on the
ground, rolled a small amount of the wet dirt around in his
fingers, and placed some of the "clay" on each of the blind
man's eyes. Jesus then commanded the man to go wash off
the mud at the pool of Siloam.

It may have seemed a strange thing to do; but when the
man exercised faith in Jesus and obeyed, he was given his
sight. Jesus told His disciples—and He is still telling us
today—that it wasn't blindness that brought glory to God,
it was healing! Nowhere in the Scriptures do we ever see
Jesus putting sickness or infirmity on anyone. Neither had
God done such a thing so His Son could demonstrate either
His power or the **Father's** power. Although veiled in human
flesh, Jesus was the image and expression of the Father.
Jesus told the people that if they had seen Him, then they
had seen the Father. If God puts sickness on people, then
sometime, somewhere Jesus would have done the same.

Even though God does not put sickness on people, has
God left us helpless before the ways of the devil and the
curse of the law? Of course not! When we acknowledge our

sin nature and confess Jesus as Savior and Lord, we receive a new nature which is the nature of God, that same nature which Adam and Eve had before the fall. Consequently, we are new creations in Christ Jesus, adopted into the family of God where **Satan no longer has a legal right to us.** Instead, we have the rights and privileges of God's kingdom which enable us to exercise authority over the devil and all his works.

So we need to know how sickness invades our bodies, don't we? If we are going to be healed, we must first be convinced that it is God's will to heal. I know a family who were committed Christians, but they were sick all the time. The children were so consistently ill that the mother joked about having a regular appointment at the doctor's every week. Then this woman was invited to one of my first Bible studies and heard the Word of healing. Soon she was convinced that healing was part of the salvation package which Jesus purchased for us at Calvary. This lady started praying the Word over her children, rebuking the enemy, and saw sickness flee every time. Years later she could say that, except for regular checkups, none of them had seen a doctor in years. She and her family learned not only how to be healed but how to walk in divine health.

Before a person is born again, Satan can load that individual with all kinds of his evil "gifts"; but when we give our lives to Jesus, we can shut the door on any package the devil wants to deliver. If you don't have the door locked, however, the devil and that sin principle will get in whenever possible. Don't forget that Satan *hates* you because you are created in God's image and likeness. Satan wants to destroy that image. When you were born again, Satan painted a bull's-eye on your back; and he is trying to get you with his fiery darts. The more committed you are to Christ, the more you serve the Lord, the more Satan wants to get you. Sickness is one of the best ways to put you out of commission. So you don't have to sin for Satan to *try* to give you sickness.

One time when I was teaching at an encounter, I walked to the pulpit and was suddenly overcome with nausea. I was just minding my own business—and God's—when suddenly I was terribly ill. You know the devil did not want me to stand before all those people and teach the delivering power of God's Word. With God-given presence of mind, I called on our singer to minister another song and slipped from the platform to look for some sort of container in which to get rid of the contents of my stomach. I spied a wastebasket just in the nick of time. Some of my staff quickly gathered around me and rebuked the sickness in Jesus' name, asked the Lord for healing, and instantly I felt God's strength flood my body. Before the singer had finished, I was sitting serenely on the platform ready to teach. Praise the Lord!

FINDING ANSWERS

Do you enjoy finding the culprit in mystery stories? Well, let's find some of the *mysterious* ways *we* leave ourselves open to sickness and ill health. Although sin doesn't have to be the reason for an attack, sin will *always* open the door to sickness. It doesn't matter what kind of sin it is, a bad attitude is no less sinful than murder. Avoid sin; but if you do sin, quickly repent and be cleansed. Shut the door on the devil! We have God's Word in I John 1:9 that, *"If we confess our sins, he is faithful and just to forgive us our sins, and to cleanse us from all unrighteousness."* Sin brings death; and sickness is death attaching itself to us, *"But if we walk in the light, as he is in the light, . . . the blood of Jesus Christ his Son cleanseth us from all sin"* (I John 1:7).

Many years ago I became very angry over a situation. A certain person had pulled some bad business deals on people in our church congregation. Although the matter had been handled, I began to meditate on it; and the more I meditated the angrier I became. Shortly after that I came down with severe flu symptoms: sore throat, temperature, etc. Of course, I rebuked the devil and rebuked the devil—without results. Can you imagine how shocked I was when the Lord said, "The devil isn't the problem; *you are.*" The Lord showed me how I had opened the door to sickness by allowing bitterness to lodge in my heart. What the person did was wrong, but I needed to leave the matter with God. Needless to say, I repented of my sin and slammed the "door" on the sickness—and received my healing!

Another way we can be attacked with sickness, disease, and infirmity is through the door of inheritance. If someone in your family tree had a disorder, some of that bad fruit may drop on you. That doesn't seem fair, does it; but the enemy will enter through any door he can. However, don't despair; the Holy Ghost can bring repair. We can lay the ax of God's Word to the root of that tree, free ourselves from any "generational curse," and stop it from bearing bad fruit in future generations:

> *And they that shall be of thee shall build the old waste places: thou shalt raise up the foundations of many generations; and thou shalt be called, The repairer of the breach, The restorer of paths to dwell in* (Isaiah 58:12).

My husband Wally and I know a man who had a very bad

inheritance. All the males in his family for several generations had heart problems. None of them had lived past their forties. That's a dire circumstance to face, isn't it? The man was married and had sons of his own, and he didn't look forward to an early death. However, this man took hold of the Word of God and came against Satan and that evil inheritance. I'm happy to say that he is "hale and **hearty**" today in his fifties, and the doctors give him a clean bill of health—all because of Doctor Jesus.

In this busy day in which we live, many of us are committing sins against our bodies without fully realizing what we are doing. We put ourselves under unnecessary stress, we often don't get enough sleep, and we don't eat properly. How many people go without breakfast, grab "fast food" for lunch, and eat "prepared" food for dinner? You wouldn't treat your dog that way! But we treat our bodies that way. That is sin! If we belong to Christ, we are part of His body and the Holy Spirit has made His home in us. That is reason enough to care properly for our bodies; we only get one in this lifetime, and it will wear out and die early if we don't take care of it. Stop and think about it; would you treat Jesus that way? I don't think so:

> . . . *Now the body is not for fornication, but for the Lord; and the Lord for the body. And God hath both raised up the Lord, and will also raise up us by his own power* (I Corinthians 6:13,14).
> *What? know ye not that your body is the temple of the Holy Ghost which is in you, which ye have of God, and ye are not your own? For ye are bought with a price: therefore glorify God in your body, and in your spirit, which are God's* (I Corinthians 6:19,20).

When God created the universe, every part was to function in harmony with every other part, and He set certain laws or principles in motion to keep it that way. Our bodies are no exception because they are part of God's universal creation. I've found that we don't operate well outside of God's principles. Unless we obey laws of good nutrition and good health, we will get run-down, sick, and be susceptible to disease. In the beginning God prepared an earth system that was compatible with our bodies: fresh air, clean water, and ground to bring forth good food. I know mankind today is ruining the ecology, but we can do our part to change this and believe the Lord to keep us healthy when we trust Him and obey His Word and His principles:

> *But if the Spirit of him that raised up Jesus from the dead dwell in you, he that raised up Christ from the dead shall also quicken your* **mortal** *bodies by his Spirit that dwelleth in you* (Romans 8:11).

Let's look at another incident in Jesus' earthly ministry which makes very clear God's will about healing. You may read the account in both Matthew 8 and Mark 1. Our Lord had been teaching and working miracles in the towns around Galilee. Because the fame of Jesus had spread through the entire region, a certain man diseased with leprosy had heard about the healer. He did what any man in his condition might do when news of a possible cure came to him. As quickly as possible the man made his way to Jesus, but this wasn't any easier for the leper than it had been for the woman with the issue of blood. Everywhere the man went he had to cry, "Unclean, unclean," because he was a leper.

No one wanted a leper around them, but this man had

enough faith to go to Jesus in spite of the people. He forged his way right into Jesus' presence, knelt before him, and pleaded, *"If thou wilt, thou canst make me clean."* Great compassion for this hopelessly diseased man filled the heart of Jesus. Without hesitation Jesus reached out his hand and touched the man saying, ***"I will; be thou clean."*** As soon as Jesus spoke those words, the leprosy left the man and his skin was fresh and new.

Most of us think leprosy was a disease of ancient times; but there are regions of the world where people are still afflicted with this dread disease, and leper colonies exist today. I'm here to tell you that Jesus' is still healing lepers! Believe it or not, I have received a testimony from a man who has been gloriously healed of this disease! In today's modern society AIDS is as incurable as leprosy was in Jesus' day. However, Jesus makes no distinction between curable and incurable, today or yesterday. I have seen several people healed of AIDS, and their healing has been documented. Glory to the Lord!

When you take Jesus as your Savior, you get the whole salvation package. In that package is deliverance, redemption, and ***healing***. The Greek word *sozo* which is translated *salvation* in the New Testament literally means "deliverance, redemption, and healing." Jesus takes your sin and gives you His righteousness. He takes your sickness, and He gives you health. He takes your death and gives you eternal life. Do you think that is a good package? Even though you lost it all in the first Adam, you regained it all in the last Adam, Jesus Christ. All the weapons which were formed against you cannot prosper (see Isaiah 54:17), because Jesus came and dismantled those weapons. Praise the Lord:

*Do not err, my beloved brethren. Every good gift and every perfect gift is from above, and cometh down from the Father of lights, with whom is **no variableness**, neither shadow of turning* (James 1:16,17).

Chapter Two

GOD WROTE THE PRESCRIPTION

What a miracle! My heart overflowed with wonder and amazement when I saw the tiny bundle the nurse was handing me. I pulled back the blanket and looked into the face of the "most beautiful" baby ever born. I cuddled the precious little girl Wally and I had named Sarah. She was truly a gift from God. For 13 years we cried out to the Lord for a child, and now the answer to our prayers was wiggling in my arms. I thought my heart would burst with love— love for her and love for God. The doctors said I could not bear children, but a man of God had prophesied a child. Wally and I had nothing but a *promise* from God and *faith*. I must confess that I had accepted our adopted son as the fulfillment of that promise, but Wally continued to believe God for a child of our flesh. And now, here she was!

Nothing is so mysteriously wonderful as new life. How can anyone see a baby and not believe in God? I've heard it said that a baby is God's promise for the future. I like that! Sarah is now a lovely young woman in her twenties; and in the years since her birth, I have seen the Lord perform miracle after miracle for childless couples, little miracles named Jordan and Joshua and Jamie and Julie! God has always been a *life giver*! No problem can ever be bigger than He is!

Did you know that the first healings that took place in the Word of God involved the healing of barren wombs? God always has wanted to prove to us that if He can give life when life is "impossible," He can certainly heal *any* life He has created. God laid the foundation for healing in the very beginning of the Bible, back in the Old Covenant. Healing for our bodies was not a new thought in the mind of God when Jesus came upon the scene. People say to me, "I don't like the Old Testament because during that period God was a harsh God of judgment and punishment; a God of discipline and not of compassion."

THE LORD OUR GOD IS ONE GOD

The Old Testament God was not an angry, vengeful Father Who looked for opportunities to "spank" His children every time they made a mistake. Jesus didn't turn to the Father one day and say, "You've had your turn; now it's my turn." The Son didn't change the Father's mind about love, compassion, *or* healing. Christ was the very expression of *the Father's love* clothed in human flesh. One way He expressed that love was by healing those afflicted with sickness and disease. I want to remind you that whatever Jesus is, the Father is also. Jesus Himself declared that He and the Father are **one** (see John 10:30).

Jesus told His disciples that to know Him was to know the Father, and yet Philip still asked to see the Father. Jesus replied:

> . . . *Don't you know me, Philip, even after I have been among you such a long time? Anyone who has seen me has seen the Father. How can you say, "Show us the Father"? Don't you believe that I am in the Father, and that the Father is in me? The words I say to you are not just my own. Rather, it is the Father, living in me, who is doing his work* (John 14:9,10 NIV).

Jesus continued by telling the group that they should know He and the Father were One by the very works which

He did. Jesus was continually healing all manner of sickness and disease. If Jesus is a healer, so is the Father!

Philip is not alone in his confusion about the "oneness" of the Godhead. Christians are often accused of worshiping three gods because we worship Jesus and the Holy Spirit, as equals with the Father. Moses, inspired by the Holy Spirit, wrote these profound words, *"Hear, O Israel: the LORD our God is one LORD"* (Deuteronomy 6:4). Does that word *one* mean only one person? The Hebrew word *achad* or *echad* used here for "one" means "united," "collect (thoughts)," "to be alike or together." Unity must involve more than one. For example, **two** people are united in **one** marriage. The *United* States of America isn't a single state, but a collection of states working together as one.

I particularly like the Hebrew definition for *one* which can mean "a collection of *thoughts.*" What an interesting and precise revelation of God the Father, God the Son, and God the Holy Spirit. They think alike! Consequently, Their purposes are united, Their words are united, and all Their actions agree. When thoughts are spoken, they become words. From the beginning God expressed His thoughts and purposes through the creative power of His Words. The gospel of John tells us God's Word, which is from the beginning, and was made manifest in flesh—***Jesus is the Word of God***. Whatever the Father thought, Jesus did. He always carried out the Father's thoughts with His actions, and the Holy Spirit provided the supernatural power. What unity, what **oneness**!

It pleases me to know that the triune God has *never* left His people helpless. Back in the garden of Eden, God provided for mankind's healing. Don't ever forget that healing for the body is as much a part of salvation as healing for the spirit and soul. After Adam and Eve sinned, God told Satan, " . . . *I will put enmity between thee and the woman, and between thy seed and her seed; it shall bruise thy head, and thou shalt bruise his heel"* (Genesis 3:15). Right then the *miracle* birth of our Savior and Redeemer was promised. We know that the serpent was the devil (Revelation 12:9) and that the Seed of the woman is Jesus (Galatians 3:16). Praise the Lord, Jesus **was born** from a virgin's womb, and at Calvary He crushed Satan's authority over our lives.

The book of Hebrews makes a lengthy comparison of the Old and New Covenants saying that in the New Covenant we have a *better* hope, a *better* testament made sure by Jesus Christ, and a *better* covenant established upon *better* promises. Nevertheless, we must not forget that the Old Covenant is the **foundation** for everything we have in the New. The New Covenant was not the result of God changing His mind. Quite the contrary, it was the fulfilling of every purpose established in the Old. Whatever fruit we are eating today comes from God's "tree of life" which has its roots in the Old Covenant. So we will look into the Old Covenant and see the provision God's people had for health and healing.

HEALING BARREN WOMBS

How and when did God make good on His promise to be a healer? As I said previously, the first Biblical accounts of healing concern persons unable to bear children. You know the devil would do what he could to keep humanity from fulfilling God's command to replenish the earth. How frustrated Satan must have been with mankind's ability to reproduce itself; he had hated even one man made in the image of God. Consider something even more serious for Satan; he had to stop the Redeemer of mankind from being born. Of course, there is no way the devil could outsmart the Lord; and every time the devil tried to stop life, God triumphed by proving He is the giver of life.

It's not at all surprising that the first couple we find in scripture who couldn't have children was Abraham and Sarah. It was Abraham who was singled out by God as the one through whom God's *Seed* would come. Abraham was a man of *75* when God first called him; and to complicate the matter, his wife Sarah had never borne children. Isn't it just like God to come to this pair and tell them they would have offspring so numerous they couldn't be counted? However, before the Lord manifested His promise of a son to Abraham and Sarah, He exercised Abraham's faith by having him pray for others who were barren.

This miracle happened in the land of Gerar where Abraham had journeyed with Sarah and all his household. (See Genesis 20.) Abraham instructed Sarah to say she was his sister and not his wife. There were no children tagging along beside Sarah to reveal the truth, so Abraham thought no one would be the wiser. Now why would he do such a thing—even though Sarah was his half sister? I'll tell you why. He did it to "save his own skin." Sarah was extraordinarily beautiful, and Abraham feared that any "red blooded" man of Gerar would want her in his harem—want her badly enough to kill a husband to get her.

Abraham was right about one thing: it wasn't just any man who wanted her; it was the king. As far as Abimelech knew, there was nothing to stop him. Sarah was Abraham's sister, right? Wrong on two counts! Sarah was Abraham's wife, and the thing Abimelech was about to do was wrong. God revealed the truth to Abimelech in a dream and said, "You're a dead man if you touch that man's wife!" Abimelech wasted no time in returning Sarah to Abraham after he received God's ultimatum, but you can be sure Abraham was "called on the carpet" for what he had done. His lie had nearly cost the king's life.

As was the custom, Sarah had been in Abimelech's harem for a number of months going through an elaborate preparation to become the king's wife. During this time it became obvious that none of the women in the royal household were getting pregnant, not even the maidservants. Even the king's *intent* to consummate a union with Sarah had closed the wombs of the women. The Lord instructed Abimelech to have Abraham pray for the women; and when Abraham prayed, they were *all* healed. God so amazes me! Here is a heathen king and a heathen people, and yet God healed these women so they could conceive. God's love reaches everywhere!

Now let's go to Genesis 21. In my imagination I hear the cry of an infant, and I see Abraham bending over Sarah who is cradling a baby in her arms. The expression on the man's face is one of great delight. Although every father should be filled with wonder at the miracle of birth, this man is looking at a *very big* miracle. Abraham was 100 and Sarah was 90. What an amazing moment in the lives of Abraham and Sarah. It is no wonder that the elderly couple are filled with awe at the product of their faith:

And being not weak in faith, he [Abraham] considered not his own body now dead, when he was about an hundred years old, neither yet the deadness of Sarah's womb: He staggered not at the promise of God through unbelief; but

was strong in faith, giving glory to God
(Romans 4:19,20).

At God's command Abraham and Sarah named their son *Isaac* which means "laughter." I believe God was reminding Abraham and Sarah that He always has the last laugh. Years before God had said to Abraham:

And I will make my covenant between me and thee, and will multiply thee exceedingly. And I will make thee exceeding fruitful, and I will make nations of thee, and kings shall come out of thee. And God said, Sarah thy wife shall bear thee a son indeed; and thou shalt call his name Isaac [laughter]: *and I will establish my covenant with him for an everlasting covenant, and with his seed after him* (Genesis 17:2,6,19).

Do you know how Abraham responded to this miraculous promise? He laughed at the possibility of having even one son. Later God refreshed Abraham's memory concerning the promise, and Sarah, who eavesdropped on the conversation, took her turn at laughing over such an incredulous possibility. But is God a healer of bodies? Yes! Is anything too hard for Him? No! The Lord visited Sarah as He had promised, and Sarah conceived. In due time she bore Abraham a son in his old age, and Abraham named his son "Laughter" (Isaac):

Is any thing too hard for the LORD? At the time appointed I will return unto thee, according to the time of life, and Sarah shall have a son (Genesis 18:14).

Barrenness followed the next two generations like a generational curse. However, God took the opportunity to prove that He, and only He, could bring to pass the promises given to Abraham for a nation and a Savior. After Isaac married Rebekah, they soon discovered that she was as barren as her mother-in-law had been. No doubt Isaac was aware of his own miraculous birth, when he prayed for Rebekah. They received a double miracle, twins named Jacob and Esau. Jacob, too, married a barren woman named Rachel, who *demanded* that he give her a child. Jacob reminded his insistent wife that he wasn't God, but she did conceive when Jacob prayed for her. Their sons were Joseph and Benjamin. Over and over God proved Himself to be the healer and life giver. In all these examples I want you to see that if God can give life, He can heal life. Surely, He can repair and maintain what He has made!

I'm impressed by the fact that God consistently answered husbands when they prayed for their wives. The Lord has given a special anointing for healing to husbands because a husband is the God-ordained head of his home. God expects healing to flow through families when husbands and fathers pray for their households. Here, in the very first book of the Bible, we have these marvelous examples given to us. I would say to husbands who are not in the habit of praying over their family members, "Don't be afraid to pray for your wives; don't be afraid to pray for your children. You'll be amazed what God will do through you."

I'm going to tell you about a wife who didn't want her husband's prayer when she needed healing. Although the lady would ask others to pray for her physical needs, she hesitated to ask her husband because she didn't think he would pray effectively. One day when this lady was ill, the Lord told her to have her husband pray for her. The Lord said He wasn't interested in how effective she thought her husband's prayers were; if she would ask her husband for prayer, then the Lord would heal her every time. It took some courage and swallowing of pride, but the lady obeyed and received her healing. Her husband always has the opportunity to pray for her now. Listen to me: mighty power is released when a husband prays.

A COVENANT OF HEALING

Some 500 years after Abraham bounced Isaac on his knee, the nation of people which God promised had become a reality. However, something had gone wrong. Instead of a mighty people serving God, they were a nation of slaves serving the king of Egypt. During a terrible famine when Abraham's offspring numbered less than 100 persons, they moved to Egypt. Abraham's great grandson Joseph, who had become Pharaoh's "right-hand man," invited the family for dinner. Four hundred years later Joseph had been forgotten by the Egyptian leaders and over a million Hebrews had been enslaved.

When Abraham's descendants remembered they were children of promise, they began to cry to Almighty God and the Lord sent Moses to be Israel's deliverer. Moses was used by God to bring plagues on Egypt until Pharaoh was finally persuaded to let God's people go. The climax came when the death angel passed through Egypt killing all the firstborn of man and beast. However, when the angel saw blood sprinkled on doorposts of the Israelites' homes, he passed over and spared all their firstborn. You see, at God's instruction Moses had told the people to kill a lamb for every household, sprinkle its blood on their doorposts, then roast, and eat the lamb. That very night Pharaoh told those Hebrew slaves to *get out*!

God had entered a blood covenant with His people which protected and healed them. A miracle took place the night nearly 2,000,000 people sprinkled the blood and ate the lamb. Those folks had lamb outside and lamb inside, and that lamb healed every sick person and strengthened every feeble one. What a beautiful picture of Jesus, our Lamb, Who heals and delivers us. The Israelite slaves had been ill fed and ill-treated, so I would guess many of them weren't in the best shape. Just think, if only ten percent of that enormous crowd needed some sort of healing in their bodies, then 20,000 people were healed at one time. Is God able to heal a multitude? Well, I guess!

Recently in Hungary I had the opportunity to see God heal a mass of people. The pastor and congregation of the church where I was teaching were very bold in God and aggressive in faith. For the last night of the meeting, this group secured a large stadium which seats 10,000 people; and it was filled. That evening I prayed for the sick, specifically those with growths, tumors, or warts. I asked all who knew they had been healed to come to the platform. When 150 people responded, I was overwhelmed. I had expected maybe ten people to come. That night God showed me I needed to enlarge my expectations. When large groups of people come together in agreement to praise and worship the Lord, there is a rich anointing to heal the masses. No situation is too big for the Lord.

There was no situation too big for God where Israel was concerned either. The trials weren't over for God's people when they left Egypt but neither were the miracles. When they reached the Red Sea, Moses parted the waters and led the Israelites across a dry sea floor just ahead of the pursuing Egyptians—who drowned when the waters closed back over them. God's people should have seen that the Lord was bigger than any problem. Nevertheless, in just a few days, the Israelites were murmuring and complaining because they had no water. That is, they had no water except the bitter water of Marah which they were unable to drink. I think the water was bitter because the people were bitter.

Here were 2 million people in a desert with no water fit to drink, but Who did they have with them? Yes, they had the Lord! He instructed Moses to cut down a tree and throw it in the water; then the water was "healed." People speculate about what kind of tree would have neutralized the bitter water, but I know it was a *miracle* tree. Just as the passover lamb typified Jesus, so the tree typified the cross of Calvary. Because of *that tree* the bitter waters of sin have been neutralized, and we can drink freely of the waters of salvation. God can heal our bodies, and He can also heal our circumstances.

It was here at Marah that the Lord gave to Israel, and to us as children of faith, one of the greatest promises of healing found in the Scriptures. When God made the water of Marah "sweet," He said to the people:

> . . . *If thou wilt diligently hearken to the voice of the LORD thy God, and wilt do that which is right in his sight, and wilt give ear to his commandments, and keep all his statutes, I will put none of these diseases upon thee, which I have brought upon the Egyptians: for* **I am the LORD that healeth thee** (Exodus 15:26).

Literally, He said, "I am your **health!**" From the moment Israel entered into a covenant of healing, they walked in health. For 38 years their shoes didn't wear out, their feet didn't swell, and they were not sick!

Do you know that God can keep you healthy? Health is far better than healing! Don't plan on getting the flu; don't plan on being sick. I have an evangelist friend who used to say, "Every winter I get the flu." And every winter she had a terrible case of the flu. The lady didn't realize she was scheduling the flu with her own mouth. When she learned that the Lord was her health and understood how her words were defeating her, she changed her "plans" and her words. No more flu! God warns that we are either justified or condemned by the words we speak. (See Matthew 12:37.)

Somehow folks tend to overlook their minds when thinking of health or healing. People just expect to suffer memory loss as they get older, but the Word says we have the mind of Christ! I'm amazed by a Christian writer whose later years were his most productive. At 70, the Lord told him the next ten years were going to be his best. He kept his same ministry schedule, traveled the world, and never took a vacation except to write. When he was 80, this man asked the Lord for another 10 years; and at 88 he wrote the best book I have ever read, except the Bible. This man *never made plans to be sick*, and he was healthy until the day he died at 90. He practiced the 3 Gs: God's grace, grit (exercise), and grain (proper eating).

Do people have to get sick to die? I don't think so! I believe that we can simply turn loose and "go home" when we are satisfied with length of days. (See Psalms 91:16.) Plan on good health throughout your entire life. The blood of Jesus doesn't lose its power or wear out as we get older. However, we must take care of our bodies just as the man I previously mentioned. Don't forget, Moses was 80 when God called him; and Deuteronomy 34:7 tells us that when he died at 120, his eyes were not dim and his natural forces were not abated.

During Moses' 40 years in the wilderness with the Israelites, he had to endure their exasperating ways. Not far from Marah the people began to murmur and grumble again. Now they were dissatisfied with God's choice of "heavenly" food, which they called manna or *"what is it?"* In their complaint they even wished to be back in Egypt where they could eat cucumbers, onions, and garlic. Those Israelites had a very short memory, didn't they? Egypt meant slavery. Because of their complaining, fire came down and destroyed many of them before they admitted their sin. Moses prayed for them, and God stopped the fire. Yes, God healed their circumstance.

However, it wasn't long before the Israelites were complaining again! They really weren't any different than people today. This time these bitter people opened the door to poisonous serpents which bit them and many died. Life was becoming a classroom for slow learners. Moses prayed for the people once more; and the Lord told him to make a brass serpent, put it on a pole, and lift it up where all those who were bitten could see it and be healed. It seems like a strange way to effect healing, but it worked:

> *And as Moses lifted up the serpent in the wilderness, even so must the Son of man be lifted up: That whosoever believeth in him should not perish, but have eternal life* (John 3:14,15).

Even Moses' own sister and brother found something about which to murmur and complain. Have you ever noticed that complainers like to complain to others and spread around their poison? These two were upset because Moses had married an Ethiopian woman. They had another complaint, also. Aaron and Miriam decided Moses wasn't the only one who should be giving orders. They claimed they could hear from God, too, and that gave them the right to share some of the leadership. As a result of her sin, Miriam became leprous. Smitten with guilt and remorse, Aaron begged Moses to pray for their sister. As a result of Moses' prayer, Miriam was healed. (See Numbers 12.)

Occasionally I telephone a friend living in another city. This person believes in divine health and healing; she has read "every" book on healing and has a library of healing tapes. However, every time we talk she has some sort of complaint. When I ask how she is, she proceeds to tell me in detail of her latest illness. "Nothing seems to be working out right for me," she will say. And nothing does. I want you to know that if you don't mix faith with God's Word and keep *your* words in line with His Word, nothing will turn out right for you either!

It wasn't the desert that created a wilderness experience for the Israelites; it was their complaining. They weren't very spiritual, and *yet God healed them.* Have you noticed that unspiritual people get healed? Even the unsaved can get healed. In Kathryn Kuhlman's meetings, the unsaved received some of the most dramatic healings. I've found that God will heal wherever faith is exercised. God is so smart! Many, many times healing brings a sinner to Christ. It doesn't have to be the other way around. Often Christians expect healing on the basis of merit instead of faith. They say, "I'm always in church, I teach Sunday school, I sing in the choir"; but God doesn't heal people who have "earned it."

WAYS AND MEANS OF HEALING

In the case of the Israelites, their sickness was the result of sin. Nevertheless, God healed them when they repented of complaining. It amuses me when sickness is sometimes referred to as a "complaint." That may be more truth than fiction. However, we know all sickness is not the result of sin. Sarah wasn't barren because of sin, and the scripture doesn't say sin brought barrenness to Rebekah or Rachel. If you are sensitive to the voice of the Holy Spirit, He will tell you when the cause of sickness is sin. Repent quickly and mend your ways, and He will mend your body.

There are times when circumstances press us into healing. Those barren women were so desperate for children that they pressed into faith and received their healing. It's natural for women to want children, and in Bible times it was a shame for a woman to be childless. Hannah was another childless woman who pressed into her answer. She promised the Lord that if He would give her a son, he would be dedicated to God. When Eli the priest agreed with Hannah's faith, she bore not one child, but six children. Hannah was faithful to her promise to God; and that first son, Samuel, was consecrated to the Lord as a small child and became one of Israel's greatest prophets.

Death stared the wife of a noted pastor in the face but she *pressed through* to life. Doctors found cancer in her liver and gave the woman no more than 3 months to live. Nevertheless, she said: "According to the Word I will live and not die!" She chose to look at God's answer rather than the symptoms or the medical report. Day after day this persistent lady spoke healing promises to her body and listened to tapes on healing. She *determined* to live and declare the works of God. It didn't happen overnight, but gradually healing came; and today the doctors can find no sign of cancer. Severe illness pressed this woman into healing, and her testimony is encouraging many others to press into God for their own healing.

Let's look at some other marvelous healings in the Old Covenant. I'm reminded of a Shunammite woman in II Kings 4:8-37 who was also barren. She and her husband befriended the prophet Elisha, who repaid the lady by praying for her to have a son. The little boy came in due time, but years later the young man died of sunstroke. Mindful of his miraculous birth, the undaunted woman saddled her donkey and went to Elisha without telling anyone of her son's death. Instead, she confessed all was well. Elisha responded to her plea for help, went to where the woman had laid her son, and prayed for his life to return. This woman, too, pressed into healing; and death was defeated.

Although the Shunammite exercised remarkable faith for the life of her dead son, I don't believe she had any faith for his birth. It was the faith of Elisha. God honors the faith of others when they pray for the sick. *You* can stand in the gap and use *your* faith for a sick person who doesn't have the necessary faith. We have prayed for people who were so ill they could not exercise faith for themselves, and we have seen them healed. Ezekiel 22:30 tells us that God searches for anyone who will fill the gap with faith so He can fulfill His will to restore rather than destroy. My Bible says believers will lay hands on the sick and they will recover! (See Mark 16:18.) How about yours?

One of the most unique healings in the Old Testament is that of Naaman the Syrian captain. Second Kings 5 describes Naaman as a mighty man in valor, *but he was a leper.* Through his little Israelite slave girl, Naaman learned of the prophet Elisha who could heal Naaman's leprous body.

The captain lost no time in getting to Israel and the prophet Elisha, who sent Naaman word to dip in the Jordan River seven times. After struggling with his pride, Naaman obeyed and was healed on the seventh dip. This Syrian was a cruel enemy of Israel, he was an idolater, and yet God desires to bring any individual to repentance through His marvelous goodness. Because of his healing, Naaman repented and accepted the God of Israel.

Through the compassion of one little slave, Naaman was no longer a leper, and neither was he an idolater. Naaman went home with healing on the inside as well as healing on the outside. What a life-changing experience! Can you imagine the joy of Naaman's little maid when she saw her master again? Her compassion and love for this man touches my heart. She had probably been captured and taken from her home to be this man's slave, and yet she cared for him. Many times in the New Testament we read that Jesus looked upon the people with compassion before He healed them. Compassion mixed with faith is a powerful combination.

On another occasion the Lord used Elisha in a most unusual way. Every time the Syrians planned a campaign against Israel, someone "tipped off" the king of Israel, and the plot was foiled. The Syrian king was furious because he supposed there was a traitor in their midst. However, one of his servants said the "informer" was Elisha, who was able to know the king's thoughts even when he was in his bedroom. The way in which the Syrian king reacted to this information always amuses me. He sent a large army after the prophet.

How the king thought his men would take Elisha by surprise, I don't know. They didn't, of course; but Elisha made no effort to escape. The prophet prayed that God would put blindness on the men, and he led the army to Israel's king Jehoram. Instead of killing the enemy, Elisha told Jehoram to feed the men and send them home—after Elisha prayed for their sight to be restored. Isn't that a unique healing? First Elisha prayed blindness on the enemy, and then he asked God to remove it.

Another healing in the Old Testament is probably the most unusual of all. It also concerns Elisha, or rather, Elisha's bones. The prophet had died and "gone to his reward," but his bones still lay in his tomb. During a battle with the Moabites some Israelite soldiers threw the dead body of a comrade into Elisha's grave. What happened next must have given the soldiers quite a fright. When the dead man's body touched Elisha's bones, the man was instantly brought back to life. So even the bones of the prophet were tremendously anointed by God! (See II Kings 13:20,21.)

You've heard of "good king" Hezekiah, haven't you? Well, the circumstances surrounding this man's healing were truly miraculous. After Isaiah the prophet came and told him to set his house in order because he was going to die, Hezekiah turned his face to the wall and beseeched the Lord for healing. Then God stopped the departing prophet "in his tracks" with the latest news bulletin from heaven: in three days Hezekiah would be healed and live another 15 years! For proof, Hezekiah asked the Lord to cause the sundial to move backward ten degrees, and God did just that!

Hezekiah was so filled with praise to the Lord that he wrote ten psalms and added to those ten another five of King David's, a psalm for every additional year of life. These are called "psalms of degrees" or "psalms of ascent." Hezekiah didn't think of the clock running down, but he saw that every year was another step closer to God. He was on an ascent to God, not a descent to death. Don't you like that kind of attitude? Just like Hezekiah, you can turn your face to the wall and cry out to God for a miracle. Then you, too, will have a song in your heart of praise to God, Who is daily drawing you closer to Himself.

Then there is "poor" Job. He was desperately ill, but Job got healed after the Lord showed him that he was self-righteous. Job confessed this sin, took his eyes off himself, and prayed for his accusing friends. With such friends Job didn't need enemies! Nevertheless, with God's viewpoint Job saw things from a different perspective; and he lived another 140 years.

Many times God heals an individual when they get free from wrong attitudes. Folks, bad attitudes are very dangerous. I know of a woman who chose to die with a heart condition rather than forgive her mother. At the same time several people around this woman were loosed from sickness by loosing bad attitudes.

God even healed a cruel pagan king when he changed his attitude. King Nebuchadnezzar was responsible for taking the Jews captive into Babylon, and yet God healed him of a nervous breakdown when he admitted an attitude of pride. Daniel warned the king that his pride would be his undoing, but he didn't listen. One day in the midst of his boasting, he suddenly thought he was an animal, and God put him out to pasture for seven years. When he finally looked up from the grass and fixed his gaze on God, his mind was completely restored. (See Daniel 4.) I want to tell you that God is still healing minds today, and he can heal your mind or the mind of someone for whom you pray.

There is a lovely woman on my staff who has been wonderfully healed of mental illness. From early childhood the lady had been in foster homes, and it was in the first foster home that she accepted Christ. However, she was not given the opportunity to grow in her newfound faith, and a great deal of trauma and abuse in other foster homes nearly obliterated her consciousness of Christ. In her teens the woman joined a pseudo-Christian cult that further obscured the truth of Christ. By her late twenties the lady was battling mental illness and was often hospitalized for both physical and emotional problems. Prompted by the Holy Spirit, the woman began reading her Bible and listening to Christian radio and TV. One morning she awoke and realized the veil over her mind had been lifted and she was completely healed. This woman is now a stable, happy person, rejoicing in Jesus her healer.

What about backsliders; will God heal backsliders? If He doesn't, then he shouldn't have healed King Jeroboam! Jeroboam was God's choice for the ten tribes of Israel at the time the kingdom divided into Israel and Judah. This king got off to a good start but "took a turn for the worse." He introduced idolatry to the nation by setting up altars to a golden calf, which the people were supposed to worship. Jeroboam feared losing his kingdom if the men of Israel went to Judah to worship God at the Temple in Jerusalem.

An unnamed prophet came to Bethel and prophesied against the golden calf which Jeroboam had erected there. When the idolatrous altar broke apart, the furious king reached out his hand to strike the prophet and instantly his hand dried up. Can you believe that Jeroboam asked this prophet to pray for his healing? I'm amazed that the prophet prayed and even more amazed that God healed this reprobate king. Nevertheless, the goodness of God leads sinners to repentance. (See Romans 2:4.) God loves backsliders, too; and He wants to heal them and draw them back to Himself.

The Lord used various means and different ways to heal in all the Old Testament situations I've mentioned. We saw that prayer healed people; activating faith was a vital part in healing; the Lord took compassion on people and they received healing; and others pressed into healing when circumstances put them under pressure. We also saw unusual and unique ways of healing such as Naaman dipping seven times in the Jordan, and even Elisha's bones gave life to a dead soldier. When the water at Marah was healed, Moses received a "word of knowledge" from the Lord (see I Corinthians 12:8) telling him to cut down the tree and place it in the water. What is God demonstrating to us? Simply, that He loves us all. He will use any means possible to bring healing to our bodies because He loves us so much! I believe all things are possible to Him, don't you?

Almost always God gives me a "word of knowledge" about someone in my meetings. Very recently the Lord told me there was someone in our service who had suffered severe headaches for several years, but He was going to heal this individual that evening. A young man responded when I told the people what the Lord had spoken to me. A terrible motorcycle accident had fractured the man's skull in several places; and while these bones were knitting, large calcium deposits formed in these areas causing constant, excruciating headaches. The congregation and I prayed for the young man, and he was instantly released from the headaches. A week later he testified that he hadn't had a sign of a headache since. Praise the Lord!

As we look at the Old Covenant, we see such wonderful healings. At one time, King David was so ill that people stayed away from him because he smelled so bad. Yes, illness can actually have a very offensive odor. David may have had his healing from this terrible illness in mind when he wrote:

> *Bless the LORD, O my soul, and forget not all his benefits: Who forgiveth all thine iniquities;* **who healeth all thy diseases**; *Who redeemeth thy life from destruction . . . so that thy youth is renewed like the eagle's* (Psalms 103:2-5).

God will also heal others when we send His healing Word to them. Psalms 107:20 says, *"He sent his word, and healed them, and delivered them from their destructions."* What a good "package" to receive, and it's even faster than the U.S. Mail.

Over and over again God provided healing for His people. I'm so thankful that the Holy Spirit has recorded these incidents and given us promises which are as good today as the day they were given. God and His Word are the same and neither ever changes. Before Christ Jesus came, every promise was made sure by the blood of a sacrifice; but now every promise has been made sure by the blood of Jesus Christ. No wonder the book of Hebrews says we have a *better promise*. Aren't you thankful that you can change the circumstance of physical illness with the unchanging Word of God? The Lord is just as concerned for you today as He has ever been for anyone.

Chapter Three
CALLING DOCTOR JESUS

The doctor shook his head in utter amazement. What he found in his examination just couldn't be. There was no way the stem of the woman's eye could be reconnected with the eyeball. Every manner of treatment, even surgery, had proven useless; and blindness had been inevitable for his patient. Nevertheless, the woman sitting in the examination chair confirmed his findings; her vision in both eyes was perfectly clear.

With no hope of recovery, except for a miracle, this woman had attended a healing service; and what doctors and medical science could not do, the Lord had done in an instant. Not only did the woman's doctor confirm in writing this remarkable healing, but she also has written confirmation from another doctor. God had taken the "im" out of impossible again! This is the kind of thing Jesus does all the time.

Since Jesus paid the price for our healing, it just makes sense to me that He would continually prove it in bodies all over the world. His love for us knows no boundaries and neither does His healing power! Although God is unlimited, for your sake and mine, Jesus suffered the limitations of a human body in order to pay the awful price for our physical healing. Isaiah foretold it, and Jesus confirmed it: "by His stripes we are healed!"

Let's look again at the prophecy given by the Lord to Isaiah concerning the healing work of the Messiah. In chapter 53 the prophet began by wondering who would believe his report, but he declared that the work is **sure**, whether it is believable or not. To this day many do not believe in the healing work of Calvary, but that makes it no less certain. There are multitudes of people who can *verify* that Jesus is a Healer.

The woman whose eyes were miraculously healed has no doubt about the healing power of her Lord:

> *Who hath believed our report? and to whom is the arm of the LORD revealed? . . . we hid as it were our faces from him; he was despised, and we esteemed him not. Surely he hath borne our griefs, and carried our sorrows: yet we did esteem him stricken, smitten of God, and afflicted. But he was wounded for our transgressions, he was bruised for our iniquities: the chastisement of our peace was upon him; and with his stripes we are healed* (Isaiah 53:1,3-5).

I'm a bit puzzled even by the Bible translators who apparently didn't believe Isaiah's report. All they could see was the payment for sin without the payment for sickness, so they translated two key words in verse 4 as "griefs" and "sorrows" instead of "sickness" and "pain". However, Matthew 8:16,17 makes it clear that healing was in the atonement because it says: *"When the even was come, they brought unto him many that were possessed with devils: and he cast out the spirits with his word, and healed all that were sick: That it might be fulfilled which was spoken by Esaias the prophet, saying, Himself took our infirmities, and bare our sicknesses."*

The Hebrew word translated "borne" in Isaiah 53:4 is *nasa* and it means "to suffer punishment for something." The word used for "carry" means "to totally carry away." Now I want to give you a very accurate rendition of this verse; "Surely He stood in our place and took the punishment for our pains and and He totally carried away our sicknesses." The next verse says, "he was wounded for our transgressions"—the sins we commit against people, "he was bruised for our iniquities''—those sins we commit against God. When you were "born again," you realized Jesus took your place and was punished for all your sin, but did you understand that He carried it all **away**?

In showing you what Jesus did with sin, I want to show you what Jesus did with sickness. Jesus carried away your transgressions and your iniquities so you would never have them anymore. Are you supposed to go back into your past and pick up the burden and guilt of your various sins? Does the Holy Spirit come to remind you of your sins, "You smoked, you drank, you took drugs," or whatever? Of course not! The Holy Spirit comes to set you free and to let you know that your sin has been carried away "as far as the east is from the west."

The "scapegoat" in the Old Covenant is a very graphic picture of what God did with sin. Leviticus 16:7-22 contains God's instruction concerning what is called the "scapegoat." Once a year on the Day of Atonement, two goats were brought to the door of the Tabernacle when the sin of the people was to be purged. Lots were cast to choose which goat was to be presented before the Lord and which goat was to be driven into the wilderness.

The first goat was killed, and its blood taken into the Holy of Holies where it was sprinkled on the Mercy Seat signifying the covering of the people's sin. Then the priest laid his hands on the living goat, confessing over the "scapegoat" all the iniquities and transgressions of the Israelites. This goat "carrying all the sin" was led into the wilderness where it was released, thus signifying that the people's sin was carried away to a place where it would never be seen again. In this manner, the Lord not only purged the sin of His people, He also *put it away.*

What a wonderful picture of what Jesus did for us at Calvary. When He died, He took the punishment each of us deserved because of sin. However, that is not all that He did; He *carried away* all our sin. Do you see that Jesus was represented by both goats in the Old Covenant? He is our "scapegoat." Jesus not only forgave your sin, but He set you *free* from your sin. The past has been forgiven and forgotten! You don't have to fear that sin is suddenly going to jump on you, because it has been driven into the sea of God's forgetfulness.

Through Christ you have been born again and given a new nature so that you can live freely in His life rather than living under the bondage of sin and death. (See Romans 8:2.) A sin nature no longer rules your life because you have made Jesus your Lord. Does that mean you can never sin again? No, your freedom of choice is never removed; but your desires have been changed. I know an evangelist who shocks his audience by saying, "I smoke all I want, I drink all I want, I lie and cheat all I want." With a remark like that, he certainly gets everyone's attention; then he quickly adds, "I just don't want to do any of those things!"

> *But if we walk in the light, as he is in the light, we have fellowship one with another, and the blood of Jesus Christ his Son cleanseth us from all sin. If we confess our sins, he is faithful and just to forgive us our sins, and to cleanse us from all unrighteousness* (I John 1:7,9).

SICKNESS HAS BEEN SENT AWAY

You may say, "I know all this regarding sin, but how does it relate to sickness?" Jesus not only took the punishment and paid the price for sickness as well as sin but He also carried sickness away in the same package with sin, so you wouldn't have to suffer from either again. Jesus is your "scapegoat" for sickness too. The Old Covenant "scapegoat" was driven so far into the wilderness that it never made its way back into the Israelites' camp, and neither is sickness supposed to come back upon you. Jesus *carried sickness away* along with your sin. Jesus took sin and sickness upon Himself in order that you might walk free of sin and free of sickness. That is truly divine health:

> *What do ye imagine against the LORD? he will make an utter end: affliction shall not rise up the second time* (Nahum 1:9).

Just as the Lord has made provision for sin committed by believers, He has also made provision for the physical ills of believers. Over and over in the Old and New Covenants, God has given us promises for the healing of our bodies. We should all be growing in the knowledge of the Lord, and that *knowledge contained in the Word* gives us greater and greater power to live a sinless life in a healthy body. However, we must exercise that power. Change your mind about sickness! Change what you say about sickness! Don't just expect to be healed if you are ill; expect to walk in health. You have the nature of the One Who is *never* sick, just as surely as you have the nature of the One Who never sins.

The apostle Paul prayed that the God of our Lord Jesus Christ, the Father of glory, might give to us the spirit of wisdom and revelation *in the knowledge of Him*. Paul wanted every believer to understand clearly the good things which God has in mind for His children, and how much benefit and blessing He has laid up in store for us. Among these benefits are healing and health. Praise the Lord, Paul didn't stop there. He continued by emphazing God's ability to give all these blessings to us, ability and power which was demonstrated when He raised Jesus from the dead. That **same** power is working for all those who believe. (See Ephesians 1:17-19.)

In case there may still be a question in your mind concerning healing as a part of the atonement, let me take you to Matthew 8:16,17. This portion of scripture describes a typical day in the life of the Lord Jesus. The people had brought many to Jesus who were either possessed by demons or who were sick in their bodies. Jesus cast out the demons with His Word, and He healed *all* the people who were ill. Notice what the Holy Spirit recorded next through Matthew, *"That it might be fulfilled which was spoken by Esaias* [Isaiah] *the prophet, saying, Himself took our **infirmities** and bare our **sicknesses.**"* This passage clearly refers to Isaiah 53:4 and shows that Jesus, in fulfilling Isaiah's prophecy, is not only our Savior but also our Healer. Without question healing for our physical bodies is in the atonement.

In this Matthew account I want you to notice that faith in Jesus' ability to heal caused people to bring others who were sick and afflicted to Jesus for their healing. The persons who needed a touch from Jesus did not come on their own. Many times in the scripture, the sick and oppressed were healed through the faith of someone else. If it happened then, it can happen today. We can stand in faith for others even when that other person is not exercising faith. That may seem preposterous, but it is true. The centurion believed for his servant (Matthew 8:5-10), Jairus believed for his daughter (Mark 5:22-24,35-43), and friends believed for the paralytic who was lowered through a roof into Jesus' presence (Mark 2:1-12). God wants us well so much that He accepts the afflicted one's faith or the faith of another on their behalf.

Years ago my mother traveled to Dallas, Texas, to hear a man who had a dynamic healing ministry. Mother was terribly burdened for my father who had suffered a nervous breakdown and was in very bad condition. When my mother stood weeping before this evangelist, he received a "word of knowledge" about the situation. "You are crying because you think your husband is demon possessed," he told my mother, "but that is not the case." He said my father was terribly oppressed and broken down. Then the man of God told my mother to take the handkerchief into which she had shed her tears and lay it on my father's body. My mother obeyed these unusual instructions and my father began to mend. The last period of my father's life was the most victorious he had ever known.

This may sound "far out" to you, but just such oddities occur in Scripture. Don't forget that the Lord is ever the same, and what He has done for one person He will do for another. Do you recall the incident in Acts 19:11,12 where God wrought *special miracles* by the hands of Paul? Handkerchiefs or pieces of cloth were taken from Paul by friends or relatives of persons who were ill. When these cloths were given to the sick, they were healed of diseases and delivered from demonic activity. Even the shadow of Peter healed the sick and afflicted. (See Acts 5:15,16.) Don't limit God! His thoughts are not limited to our thoughts and neither are His ways. (See Isaiah 55:8.) Open your heart and your mind to everything the Lord has for you.

REDEEMED FROM THE CURSE OF THE LAW

Previously, I pointed out that when sin entered the human experience, sickness came with it. It is only reasonable that when Jesus took care of the problem of sin, He also took care of the problem of sickness; they came in the same package. Sickness was the effect of sin. God warned His people in the Old Covenant that sin brought sickness, but obedience brought health and healing. Deuteronomy 28, in outlining those things that come as a result of sin, calls this "the curse of the law." All manner of illness is mentioned in this passage as well as other calamities. As sinners we were under the curse of the law. However, Jesus took the curse upon Himself at Calvary. (See Galatians 3:13.) Christ redeemed you and me from everything related to the curse and that includes sickness.

The word *redeem* means to "buy back." Jesus bought us back when we were in the "slave market" of sin. He paid the price for the redemption of our lives with His own perfect life. The word *redemption* comes from the word *redeem*. If I buy something, I have purchased it and it then belongs to me. No one else can lay claim to what I have bought. However, *redeem* means much more than simply buying an object; it means "to repossess" that object through purchase. Humanity originally belonged to God; we were His creation and His possession, created for His pleasure.

Then Adam's all-encompassing "error" gave the devil possession of something that truly wasn't his. Satan proceeded to abuse, misuse, and ruin God's perfect product until no one would want it but an ever-loving and compassionate Maker. He saw the possibility of restoring His creation to its original state and original condition. So God set in motion a plan to "buy back" that which was so priceless to Him—but the price tag was His priceless Son. The transaction was completed at Calvary, where the Lord

redeemed you and me and reinstated us as His own.
Let's see what God bought back:

> *What? know ye not that your **body** is the temple*
> *of the Holy Ghost which is in you, which ye have*
> *of God, and ye are not your own? For ye are*
> *bought with a price: therefore glorify God in your*
> ***body**, and in your spirit, which are God's*
> (I Corinthians 6:19,20).

Where does the Holy Spirit live; where are you supposed
to glorify God? In your body! Does the Holy Spirit want to
live in a dump? Of course not. How can you glorify God in
your body? There are several ways, but being well and
staying well is of prime importance in giving God glory
through your body. You are made in His image and likeness,
so let the world see what God is like. Be healed!

Most Christians have no difficulty believing that they are
redeemed in their souls as well as their spirits; but when
it comes to physical redemption, many have a problem
believing. However, it is only reasonable that redemption
is for the whole person. You are a three-part being—spirit,
soul, and body; and God intends for you to be like Him in
every area of your being. I'm sure you want to glorify the
Lord by demonstrating His likeness in your mind, in your
spirit, *and in your body*.

One part of your being is no less important to the Lord
than another. You have been redeemed in body as well as
spirit and soul. Whatever you are going to do for God in
this world is going to be done while you are in your body.
Of course, every believer will receive a resurrection body
at the resurrection—a body which will not be subject to
corruption and death. In the meantime, the Lord has made
provision for you to live in a body that can be healthy and

strong. You have authority over sickness and disease that attempts to invade your body or the body of another. Exercise that right and privilege. (See Luke 10:19.)

Not long ago a couple in our church took a transient into their home because he had no place to go. When the young man became ill, the couple sent him to the doctor. To their dismay, tests revealed that the young man had AIDS. Anger boiled in the heart of the man who had so graciously given a home to an individual who now threatened the health and even the lives of his family. This man's first thought was to order his "guest" out of the house.

Before the man could say anything, the Holy Spirit spoke in his heart, telling him to spend his anger on the disease and not on the young man who was so ill. Forcefully, and with authority, the man commanded AIDS to leave the house and never return. Many months and several tests later, there is no sign of AIDS in the young man's body. Why? Because Jesus paid the price for his healing, and one man exercised his authority in Christ!

Isn't Jesus the Word made flesh? Well, Psalms 107:20 says that God sent His Word and healed *you*. Jesus assuredly paid for your physical body with His own physical body in the work of redemption. He said that He would die in your place for your sins, and He carried away those sins. He said that He would take stripes on His back for your sicknesses. Not only did He carry away your sin but He also carried away your sickness. When the Word says God did something, it was obviously His will to do it. Therefore, I know it is the will of God to heal our bodies. Otherwise, Jesus would not have taken those stripes for our healing.

I've heard people say that even though God is willing to heal, it is obvious that not all people get healed; so in some cases God must have a reason for not healing. To substantiate their argument they may say that God is not willing for anyone to perish, but we know there are people perishing every day. That's right, but did Jesus pay the full price for sin so that not one soul should ever have to go to hell? Yes, He did—so that isn't God's choice; it's an individual choice, either through ignorance or willful rejection.

Jesus paid the full price for your healing and God wants you to take it. He doesn't want you ignorant about what is yours in Christ; He wants you to receive what is yours by choosing to accept it.

I want to share a testimony in which a choice made the difference. A woman wrote and told me how the Lord had healed her body as a result of watching my TV program "Today With Marilyn." At the point where I prayed for the sick, she thought, *"Why not!"* She prayed with me, laying her hands in the area of her back and kidneys where she was suffering severe pain. In her own words, "No one this side of Heaven could ever know how badly I hurt for ever so long." The constant pain persisted even after prayer, but this woman continued to stand on her choice to be healed. When she awoke the next morning, all the pain was gone! The letter concluded, "Jesus must surely understand our hurts, and He shows compassion. I thank Him for taking all that pain on Himself." Praise the Lord, this woman's healing was just a choice away.

GOD IS MERCIFUL AND FULL OF COMPASSION

Why does God want to heal His people, and how has He demonstrated that willingness? Undoubtedly, the best expression of the Father's will is seen in the life of Jesus;

but God didn't wait until Jesus ministered healing to tell His people why He wants them to be healthy in body. Although there are words and "pictures" throughout the Old Covenant which express God's desire to heal, Micah 7:18,19 wonderfully sums up the reason:

> *Who is a God like unto thee, that pardoneth iniquity, and passeth by the transgression of the remnant of his heritage? he retaineth not his anger for ever,* **because he delighteth in mercy.** *He will turn again,* **he will have compassion upon us;** *he will subdue our iniquities; and thou wilt cast all their sins into the depths of the sea.*

Our God is merciful and compassionate. Illness, for any reason, does not please Him. It never delights the Lord to see His people sick. He delights in mercy, and His compassion for us causes Him to take action. God took action first in the Garden of Eden when He slew a lamb, sprinkled its blood, and covered Adam and Eve. I know the Bible doesn't say it was a lamb, but I believe it was because that sacrificed animal was the first "picture" we have of Jesus, the Lamb Who was sacrificed for us.

In every Old Covenant feast or religious ordinance, a picture of Jesus can always be found. Let's look again at the events concerning the Passover where Jesus is beautifully portrayed in the Passover lamb. When a "perfect" lamb without a spot or blemish was killed for each family in Israel, it wasn't just the blood that brought about deliverance. Although that blood on the doorposts caused the death angel to pass over those homes, it was the lamb which the people ate that healed every sick and feeble person among them. Jesus, our "Passover Lamb" is both Savior and Healer.

Another Old Covenant "picture" of Jesus is found in the cleansing of lepers. Even in those days lepers could be healed. It wasn't medically possible, but it was possible with God. The healed leper would bring two birds to the priest, who would kill one bird. When the living bird was dipped in the blood of the dead bird, it would be released to fly away. Then with some of the blood and oil, the priest would "anoint" the leper's right ear, thumb, and big toe. After this procedure the priest would pronounce the leper clean. Once again, we see Jesus pictured in the two birds; in death He shed His blood for our sin, but He also carried away that sin.

One of the most graphic pictures of Jesus and His redemptive work at Calvary is seen in the brazen serpent which Moses lifted up on a pole in the midst of the Israelites. Did looking at that serpent forgive sins, or did it heal bodies? It healed bodies! I do believe God forgave the people of their murmuring when they were willing to look at the brazen serpent, but the purpose for the serpent was to effect healing in those who had been bitten by poisonous snakes.

Repeatedly in the Old Covenant, God demonstrated His mercy and compassion by healing people. God is telling us through these examples that He wants people whole in body as well as in spirit because He loves and cares for everyone. Then . . . *when the fullness of the time was come, God sent forth his Son, made of a woman, made under the law. To redeem them that were under the law,* . . . (Galatians 4:4,5). Although Jesus was perfectly human, He was also perfectly divine, an exact picture of the Father; and in everything the Son did, the Father was demonstrated. Not once but many times, the Word says that Jesus ministered to people's needs because He was moved with compassion. If Jesus was moved with compassion, so was the Father; and the Holy

Spirit in Jesus fed hungry stomachs, *healed sick bodies*, and raised the dead.

Although wholeness and healing for the body was nothing new with the coming of a new covenant, the new is better. Whatever benefits and privileges belonged to God's people in the Old Covenant, we now have in a greater and more perfect dimension because we no longer look for a Redeemer in types and shadows. We now see Jesus clearly, the One Who made the ultimate sacrifice through the shedding of His own blood. Before Jesus' death and resurrection, sin was only covered; but when Jesus "signed" a new testament with His blood, sin and sickness were put away. If the Old Testament had been the best, there would have been no need for a better one:

> *For if that first covenant had been faultless, then should no place have been sought for the second* (Hebrews 8:7).

If God healed in the Old Testament, is He going to heal in the New Testament? Obviously, the answer is, "yes." If God healed in the New Testament, is He going to heal today? Hebrews 13:8 reveals Jesus as the One Who is the same yesterday, *today,* and forever. Therefore Jesus is healing today, and He will continue to heal as long as there are sick bodies to heal. If the God of the Old Covenant healed because of mercy and compassion, He is healing today because of mercy and compassion. How do I know? Again and again the book of Psalms and other scriptures declare that God's mercy endures forever:

> *It is of the LORD's mercies that we are not consumed, because his compassions fail not. They are new **every** morning: great is thy faithfulness* (Lamentations 3:22,23).
>
> *O give thanks unto the LORD; for he is good; for*

his mercy endureth for ever (I Chronicles 16:34).

What moved Jesus to heal? Over and over the Word says compassion moved Him to heal the sick and deliver those who were demonized. The Greek meaning for *compassion* is "to be deeply stirred or moved from within." Quite literally Jesus was *moved* with compassion. When Jesus healed the leper who fell at His feet begging to be healed, the plight of the man caused Jesus to be moved with compassion; and He expressed His will by healing the man. (See Mark 1:40-42.) I must add that the man had faith to be healed. If God's compassion were the only requirement for healing, every person alive would be well and healthy. Yet if we have the faith, God always has the compassion.

It isn't difficult for people to have compassion on those who are sick; but when individuals demonstrate demonic activity, people are more often moved with fear or disgust rather than compassion. However, this was never Jesus' response to the demonized; He always responded with compassion. After delivering the man of Gadara who had a legion of demons, Jesus told the man to go home to his friends and tell them of the great thing the Lord had done for him because He had compassion on him. (See Mark 5:19.)

Jesus was moved with compassion when He saw the weary multitudes who were scattered as sheep without a shepherd (see Matthew 9:36). Jesus' compassion moved Him to heal the sick among those multitudes of people, and compassion moved Jesus to feed a hungry crowd more than once. The compassion of our Lord caused Him to give sight to two blind men from Jericho, and compassion for a widow woman who had lost her son caused Jesus to stop a funeral procession and raise the young man from the dead (see Luke 7:13).

Many, many times the writers of the gospels recorded the compassion of Jesus which moved the Lord to continually minister deliverance to those oppressed by sickness and demons. Jesus Himself, in telling the story of the prodigal son, emphasized the compassion of this young man's father in welcoming him back home and reinstating him to the position of son and heir, which the prodigal had forfeited (see Luke 15:20). Do you realize that Jesus is illustrating the love of our heavenly Father for His wayward children? Without the anointing of the Holy Spirit, Jesus could have healed no one; so, obviously, the Holy Spirit is just as compassionate as both the Father and the Son. I believe compassion is the "emotion" of love which activates God's love.

Does God want His compassion to flow through you just as it flowed through Jesus? Absolutely. If you do not have compassion for people, then you are not going to be effective in ministering to others. Jesus spoke to **every** believer when He said:

> *Verily, verily, I say unto you, He that believeth on me, the works that I do shall he do also; and greater works than these shall he do; because I go unto my Father* (John 14:12).

Look at this! The same Holy Spirit Who empowered Jesus has come to reside in you, and He is able to perform even greater works through the members of Christ's Body—when we are moved with His compassion:

> *For ye had compassion of me in my bonds, and took joyfully the spoiling of your goods, knowing in yourselves that ye have in heaven a better and an enduring substance* (Hebrews 10:34).
> *Finally, be ye all of one mind, having compassion*

one of another, love as brethren, be pitiful, be courteous (I Peter 3:8).

Seldom have I ever been so touched with compassion than when I looked at the arms of a 16-year-old Russian girl. I felt as though my "heart" would tear out of me when I learned of the "mis"fortune which had befallen Natasha. Both her arms were horribly scarred where obscenities and blasphemies had been carved by demons. Yes, demons! Natasha's mother had invited Gypsy fortune tellers to read their "fortunes," and from that time the writings were painfully cut into Natasha's arms by invisible personalities. A young man, *moved with compassion* for Natasha, brought her to one of my first meetings in Russia.

Natasha gave her heart to Jesus when she heard the good news of salvation. In the authority of Jesus' name, we bound the spirits that were using those precious arms for tablets and commanded that they never do so again. The next time I went to Russia, I was met by a lovely young woman who handed me a beautiful bouquet of flowers. Yes, it was Natasha. She held out both arms and I saw that there was little evidence of the awful cuts. The Lord had not only healed her arms, he had delivered her from the demons. I've seen Natasha several times since then, and she is living her life for the Lord Jesus Christ. My husband Wally says that we came close to having another child; because I was so moved with love and compassion for this young girl, I could easily have brought her home with me.

THE ANOINTING BREAKS THE YOKE

I have noticed that healing always comes by the power of the Holy Spirit:

. . . God anointed Jesus of Nazareth with the Holy

Ghost and with power: who went about doing good, and healing all that were oppressed of the devil; for God was with him (Acts 10:38).

The Father heals because He is merciful and compassionate, and the Son heals because He does what the Father does. However, Jesus doesn't heal just by the Father's love and compassion; He heals by the *anointing*. The Word says Jesus didn't heal the sick until after He was anointed with the Holy Spirit. (See Mark 1:10,11.)

Jesus was endued with power from the Spirit of God; that power or anointing was what healed and delivered. Did you know the Father promised the same anointing for those who are born again? Jesus, referring to this anointing as the baptism with the Holy Ghost, commanded that every believer receive it. That anointing came for the first time on the day of Pentecost; and Peter afterward declared the same experience is for us, our children, and to all that are afar off, *even as many as the Lord our God shall call.* (See Acts 1:4,5,8; 2:1-4,38,39.)

The anointing brings healing because the anointing breaks the yoke of Satan's bondage:

*And it shall come to pass in that day, that his burden shall be taken away from off thy shoulder, and his yoke from off thy neck, **and the yoke shall be destroyed because of the anointing*** (Isaiah 10:27).

The apostle Paul was very much aware that it was the anointing that gave him the power to accomplish anything for God. In Romans 15:17-19 Paul carefully gave the Spirit of God credit for any and all of the mighty signs and wonders that were manifested through him as he preached the gospel.

God always wants to confirm His Word with healing and deliverance, evident products of the power and anointing of the Holy Spirit. The Lord yearns for you to receive His anointing and to work miracles through your hands. He has promised believers that they shall lay hands on the sick and they (the sick) shall recover. Quoting Jesus, Mark wrote:

And these signs shall follow them that believe; In my name shall they cast out devils; they shall speak with new tongues; They shall take up serpents; and if they drink any deadly thing, it shall not hurt them; **they shall lay hands on the sick, and they shall recover** (Mark 16:17,18).

The anointing of the Holy Spirit does much more than heal bodies as the above scripture attests. It breaks every yoke and enables us to walk, not only in health, but in full vigor. I continually confess that according to Romans 8:11 the Spirit of Him Who raised up Jesus from the dead dwells in me, and He Who raised Christ from the dead is quickening my mortal body by His Spirit that dwells in me. There is nothing quite so valuable as personalizing the promises of God. At a recent meeting where I was speaking, I really needed the quickening and invigorating power of the Holy Spirit in my body, and I was ever so grateful for that promise.

The evangelist who held the meeting is a very vibrant man who enjoys fellowship. After the first evening meeting which lasted until 11:00 p.m., I planned to refresh my body with a good night's rest since I was the morning speaker. However, a time of food and fellowship was planned after the service, and I didn't retire until after 2:00 a.m.! A time of fellowship was planned for the ministry people between each of the services, and I thought I was being "revived to a rag," one of my husband's favorite expressions.

I looked around at the rest of the people and thought, "Isn't this getting to them?" but they looked and acted refreshed, and I realized I was being refreshed as well. The Holy Spirit was quickening my mortal body. Now, I don't recommend that anyone "burn the candle at both ends"; proper rest is part of taking care of the body. However, in the fellowship of the Holy Spirit and in the midst of ministering under the anointing, we had all been refreshed rather than exhausted. The Lord will sustain you physically in all kinds of situations and circumstances when necessary. He will quicken *your* mortal body.

We've seen that Jesus healed all manner of sickness among the people because of compassion and because of the anointing. However, the religiously "pious" objected because He didn't do it the "right" way; He healed on the Sabbath. Does sickness take a day of rest? I've never noticed that it does. People come to church sick and hurting—and Jesus heals them! I found seven places in the gospels where Jesus healed on the Sabbath: He healed the impotent man, the man born blind, the demoniac in Capernaum, He healed Peter's mother-in-law, the man with the withered hand, the woman bowed together, and He healed the man with dropsy.

It doesn't matter who you are or where you are, Jesus wants to heal you. It doesn't matter if it's a common cold or a terminal cancer, Jesus wants to heal you. Our Lord is no respecter of persons and He is no respecter of disease. You don't have to be a preacher, a Sunday school teacher, or give half your income to the church to get ready for healing. You just have to believe that He has enough love, enough compassion, and enough power to do it for *you*. In Jesus' day the people accepted healing, but the "religious" didn't believe He could forgive sin. Today people believe He can forgive sin, but they question His healing power. Why not accept both? It's not only scriptural, but it's being proven in the lives of men, women, boys, and girls every day.

One day on the outskirts of Jericho a blind man came to Jesus for the restoration of his sight. However, before he came, he *overcame* several obstacles. The man was just one in a multitude of people; would Jesus see Him? When the man called to Jesus, those around him told him to ''shut up''; would he listen to them, would Jesus hear him? The man wore a brightly colored robe which identified him as a blind person and gave him the right to beg for a living; would he throw away his ''security blanket'' and reach out to Jesus for a new life of faith and wholeness? The answer was yes to all those questions, and Bartimaeus received his healing that day. Today I want you to lay aside all the obstacles in your life and circumstances that hinder you, and believe Jesus. He will heal you if you need healing, and He will use you in healing others. *You* can have His compassion, and *you* can have His anointing!

Chapter Four
GOD IS LOVE

"The Love Bug Will Get You if You Don't Watch Out!" Did you ever hear that old tune which was a popular hit years ago? It was a "light hearted" little jingle about love and romance, but the truth it conveyed is as old as humanity. If nothing else will get to you, love will. Love has changed the course of history; kings have given up their thrones for the love of their ladies; warriors have died on the battlefield for the love of country; courageous men, women, and children have given up their lives for someone they loved; even animals have performed heroic feats to rescue a beloved master. Love is the most powerful force on earth. **God is love!**

I was so touched by the testimony of a woman recently healed in our church service. This woman had three major things wrong with her back, but she had never reached out with any confidence to receive healing. Why had she not done this when she attends a church where healing is preached and where people are prayed for in nearly every service with great results? I'll tell you why. The enemy had convinced this woman that her back would never be healed because she was not "worthy" to receive healing.

That old lie makes me so angry! I want to get up and punch the devil in the nose. However, we wrestle **not** with flesh and blood but with principalities and powers in the spirit realm. (See Ephesians 6:12). We have a weapon that will whip the devil every time, and that weapon is the Word of God. The evening the woman was healed I was teaching on the love and compassion of God to heal. As the lady *heard* God's love letter to her, faith and confidence rose in her heart and she reached out to Someone Who loved her,

Someone Who had covered her with His worthiness—and she was healed. Oh, the love of God is so powerful! I'll tell you, that evening the devil did get a "bloody nose."

I believe every person at some time in their life wonders Who God is, wonders what He is like. Civilizations around the world have "worshiped" an ugly ferocious god who is vindictive and cruel or a god who plays with people like chess pieces or a god who is totally disinterested in his creation. Some societies have imagined many, many gods; and some deify dogs, cats, snakes, and even *flies*. The most twisted lie, so close to the truth, is that *each person is god*. What a case of mistaken identity!

If none of these things are true, then what *is* God really like? Is it possible to actually know His nature, His essence, His character? Since no man has seen God at any time, how can we discover Who and What God is? The only way is to know what God says about Himself. God says that He is love. God, the Holy Spirit, inspired the apostle John to pen these words:

> *Beloved, let us love one another: for love is of God;*
> *and every one that loveth is born of God, and*
> *knoweth God . . . **God is love**; and he that dwelleth*
> *in love dwelleth in God, and God in him*
> (I John 4:7,16).

We often say that God is power or that God is healing or that God is provider. Not really; God is love. Out of His love comes power, comes healing, comes provision. Out of God's love came creation and every other thing which He has ever done or ever will do. All these things describe the acts of God, but His character is love. The fact that God is eternal, omnipotent (all powerful), omnipresent (everywhere present), and omniscient (all knowing), describe the "What" of God; but love describes the "Who" of God.

Oh yes, God is all these other things; but it is all summed up in love.

Since God is love, it is impossible for you not to be loved by Him. Just as surely as God exists, His love is being poured out on you. Right now you may think there are certainly a lot of things getting in the way of God's love, but I want you to know that God's love for you penetrates any barrier. There are no obstacles too big for the love of God. His love is constant, intense, and irrevocable. God loves sinners; God loves saints. He loves you when you are productive and when you are unproductive; He loves you when you are living victoriously and when you are living in defeat. God loves you unconditionally!

God is not like Santa Claus; His gifts are for you when you are "bad" and when you are "good." There is no doubt that faith in a righteous heart is more active than faith in a guilty heart; but in whatever condition an individual finds himself, it is our loving God's desire to heal. Jesus paid the price for our healing and God would be unjust if He did not heal each one who believes for healing. I previously said there are no barriers to God's love, but you and I *can* put up barriers that rob us of our healing. I challenge you to discover any of your own personal barriers to God's healing work. The woman who finally received healing in her back had a barrier of "unworthiness." That hindrance melted in the warmth of God's love.

If you are a parent, you want your children to be healthy. When they are sick, you never want them to get sicker. You do everything in your power to bring about healing. You take them to the doctor; you give them prescribed medicine; you do whatever is necessary. Parents love their children and want no calamity to overtake them. Loving parents would rather be sick themselves than see their children sick. Most parents would take their child's sickness upon themselves if that were possible. That is exactly what our heavenly Parent did; He took our sickness upon Himself, and then He carried it away.

Are you thinking that the Father did exactly the opposite when He put our sickness upon His Son Jesus? Don't forget that Jesus and the Father are One. They share divinity, and They shared in purchasing healing for Their children. Whatever Jesus suffered for you and me to pay the price for healing, the Father suffered also. Although Jesus is the One Who came from the Father, the Trinity endured the pain and the agony of the Cross "together." I know it grieved the Father to turn His back on Jesus, and it grieved the Holy Spirit when He had to leave Jesus at His death. They were in that thing together!

THE WAYS AND MEANS OF GOD

God is so intent on healing us and making us whole that He has a myriad of ways to do it. I've found 17 different ways in which God heals. Why does He use so many different ways; wouldn't only one way be better? Although one way might seem simpler, I may have the answer to the question. If God healed in only one fashion, somebody would say, "Well, I just don't believe God heals that way," and they would miss out. For example, if healing came only through the anointing with oil, someone might say, "That's a Presbyterian way, and I'm not Presbyterian."

If God healed only through prayer cloths, there would be those who considered that to be the Pentecostal way; if healing came only by speaking the Word, that might leave everyone out but the Baptists. Don't you see that the Lord wants to heal us any "way" possible? Don't misunderstand; I'm not saying these methods of healing are limited strictly to the groups I mentioned, but I am making a point. We are all so varied in our personalities, backgrounds, and experiences that God meets us wherever we are. God is certainly not limited in the methods He uses to heal.

Let's not put a limit on God's healing ability. God says, "If my children can't receive anointing, then maybe they will receive the Word; if they can't receive the laying on of hands, then maybe they will receive a prayer cloth." In any case the Lord "bends over backwards" to find a way in which we will receive His healing power. I'm convinced that when any person understands the love of God, he or she is stripped of all arguments; and love will change the heart—and the body.

THE ANOINTING IS STILL HERE

The first manner of healing I want to discuss is anointing. The Word tells us God anointed Jesus of Nazareth with the Holy Ghost and with power. After that anointing, Jesus went about doing good and healing everyone who was oppressed of the devil because God was with Him (see Acts 10:38). I looked up the word *oppressed* and found that it means "to dominate or exercise lordship." When Jesus healed people, He exercised His authority over Satan's domination and "Lorded it over" sickness.

When you are sick, you are being oppressed or dominated by illness; because the Word says all those whom Jesus healed were oppressed of the devil. If sickness was the oppression of the devil when Jesus was here, it is still the oppression of the devil. Remember, it was Satan who set sickness in motion in the first place. It was he who poisoned the mainstream of human life at the beginning. Sickness, infirmity, and disease of any kind is the oppression or domination of the devil. It is *always* his work:

> *Forasmuch then as the children are partakers of flesh and blood, he [Jesus] also himself likewise took part of the same; that through death he might destroy him that had the power of death, that is, the devil; And deliver them who through fear of death were all their lifetime subject to bondage* (Hebrews 2:14,15).

Jesus came to set at liberty those who were bruised because of Satan's bondage. Jesus Himself, after reading from the scroll of Isaiah, declared to the people in the synagogue that He was the One *anointed* to do this work; and He proved it by healing all manner of sickness. (See Luke 4:18.) If today you are suffering in some area of your body, Satan is exercising lordship over you; if you have cancer, it is dominating you; if you have AIDS, that thing has you bound. But praise **THE LORD** the anointing breaks the yoke! Jesus has the power to free anyone who is under the lordship of Satan because Jesus is LORD:

> *The Spirit of the Lord GOD is upon me; because the LORD hath anointed me to preach good tidings unto the meek; he hath sent me to bind up the brokenhearted, to proclaim liberty to the captives, and the opening of the prison to them that are bound* (Isaiah 61:1).

I have good news for you! Jesus has done all that the Word said He would do. Jesus, the anointed of God (Christ), opened the prison doors and released those who were taken captive in their bodies through sickness of any sort. The doors are still open; healing is available for you 2,000 years later. Read I John 3:8 and you will find, " . . . *For this purpose the Son of God was manifested, that he might destroy the works of the devil.*" Jesus took Lordship over sickness at Calvary when He loosened and broke the works of the devil. There's no doubt that sickness is still around; but its power has been broken, and Jesus is still healing bodies today.

Many believe that healing is not for our day. They say that the purpose for healing in Jesus' life and ministry was to authenticate His divinity; they say healing was one of the proofs that He was God. When faced with the fact of healing in the early Church, these people say that healing power was only manifested through the original apostles because they walked with Jesus. Or they say that the healing ministry was for the purpose of getting the Church established.

I heard a young pastor and theologian tell how God had transformed his mind and his heart about healing. He called himself a "cessationist" because he adamantly believed all miracles and healing had ceased. He read everything he could to substantiate his opinion and keep his mind bolted shut. Then this man accepted an invitation to speak at a meeting in a church where the pastor held the same opinion—he thought. The closed-minded man found himself sharing the podium with a certain well-known "fundamentalist" who has stepped mightily into the healing arena. The theologian found himself a captive audience to his views—and his experiences. Up until this time the "cessationist" had never seen a healing; but that day he not only heard the Word *in truth,* he saw the healing power of Jesus on an anointed man break the bondage of sickness. Today this pastor is telling everyone who will listen that Jesus is healing bodies today.

My Bible says that the *anointing* breaks the yoke. Jesus was able to heal because He was anointed with the Holy Spirit. It was the presence of God, the Holy Spirit, on Jesus Who performed the healing work. Jesus is now in Heaven with the Father, but Jesus sent the Holy Spirit back to earth with that same anointing to heal the sick. Listen to Jesus' own words in John 14:16, *"And I will pray the Father, and he shall give you another Comforter, that he may abide with you for ever."*

Since the Holy Spirit is here representing Jesus, Who is ever the same, yesterday, today, and forever, I know that God is still healing people today. We, too, are Jesus' representatives; and that same anointing is here for believers, enabling them to exercise authority over sickness in the lives of others. If God were to remove His power to heal, He would have to remove His power to save. I don't think anyone would "buy" that.

Other people, although they acknowledge that healing is for today, believe that God sovereignly excercises His right to use sickness as a means for drawing people to Him. I don't want any of you to "buy" that line either. Although I have dealt with this issue earlier, it bears mentioning here. This idea is such a subtle attack on the finished work of Calvary. If sickness could draw people to God and make them love Him more, then the entire world would know and love God. People everywhere are sick with something or another, and I don't see them flocking to God because of sickness. I know of more persons who **don't** love God because they've been told He puts sickness on people.

When I am sick, my body doesn't want to worship and praise the Lord. I don't have the energy to read my Bible and pray when I'm feeling sick, and I don't think I love God more when I'm sick. Yes, "the spirit is truly ready, but the flesh is weak" (see Mark 14:38). Do you get out of a sick bed, full of enthusiasm to go to your neighbor and share the love of Christ? Do you jump out of that bed on Sunday morning and say, "I can hardly wait to get to church"? Personally, I want to roll over and pull the covers over my head. Instead, however, I do get up, go to church, receive anointing, and walk out whole. Hallelujah!

One of our pastors received a note from a lady who shared a remarkable testimony of healing. At Happy Church we pray over prayer cloths, knowing that the Lord anoints them with His healing power. One of our members took a prayer cloth to her boss who had been diagnosed with cancer, and the boss was completely healed of the disease! Although the woman's boss does not attend our church, she wants to come and give this testimony. What broke the bondage of cancer in her body? It was the anointing.

THE WORD BRINGS HEALING

Another way that healing is ministered is by sending the Word. Psalms 107:20 says, *"He sent his word, and healed them, and delivered them from their destructions."* I agree with the psalmist who continued in verse 21, *"Oh that men would praise the LORD for his goodness, and for his wonderful works to the children of men!"* Just think, God loves us so much that He gave us His Word, and that Word has healing power. The Word has mighty creative force; with the Word of His power, God spoke the worlds into being.

You can find many occasions in scripture when Jesus didn't go to the sick; He simply spoke a Word of healing and the individuals were made well. Once when Jesus was teaching in Cana, a nobleman from Capernaum came to

Jesus and begged Him to go and heal his son who was at the point of death. This situation was critical; time was of the essence. Instead of going to Capernaum, Jesus said, *"Go thy way; thy son liveth."* The father believed Jesus, went home, and found his son well—healed at the very moment Jesus sent His Word to him.

Can you send the Word to heal sick bodies today? Yes, God's Word has the same dynamic power to heal today as it has ever had. The first time I really took hold of this promise was when my mother was told she had a brain tumor. We were out of town when I received the news that x-rays indicated the growth. Fear tried to grip my mind; my mother was alone, and we weren't there to pray for her. I was desperate; I felt I had to do something. Then the Holy Spirit brought to mind, "He sent His Word and healed them."

Immediately I formed a mental picture of that Word, like an arrow, piercing my mother's brain. Then I saw the arrow strike a dark spot, and the thing just exploded. I declared my faith and believed that God's Word had delivered my mother from that devilish destruction. I called my mother when Wally and I returned home, and I asked her to go to the doctor for another x-ray. You know that whatever God does can be authenticated. This x-ray came back with no sign of a tumor on my mother's brain. Glory to God! I sent the Word, and it brought healing.

Praise the Lord, the Word never wears out or loses its power! At our church we are continually sending the Word. Prayer warriors "man" a prayer line where the Word is sent into every situation that prompts a call. The ministry is also flooded with prayer requests through the mail, and our staff prays over each one, sending the Word to every need. On my TV program I always send the Word to heal sick bodies.

How I wish I could share all the miraculous testimonies of healing we receive, but here is just one. A woman, scheduled for surgery to remove a large ovarian cyst, called our prayer line. A prayer warrior prayed with her. Before the surgery she was reexamined, and the cyst was gone. She wrote back giving praise to the Lord for her healing.

Speaking the Word is another way in which healing comes; not *sending* the Word but *speaking* the Word. I've observed several evangelists who move in healing and miracles. They just say something like, "Be well in Jesus' name," or "In Jesus' name be whole," and the people are healed. Healing doesn't come because a person prays and begs forever. Jesus said prayer isn't answered because it is long or fancy. Unbelievers expect to be heard because they pray long prayers. Prayer that is answered contains faith and power— Word power. (See Matthew 6:7.)

Did Jesus heal this way? Look with me at John 5:8. To the infirm man at the pool of Bethesda, Jesus simply said, *"Rise, take up your bed, and walk."* When the Lord asked the man if he wanted to be well, the man began to give all the reasons why he wasn't. I think Jesus thought, "Spare me the details, I'm going to make you well." Jesus didn't pray a lengthy prayer; He just spoke the Word, and the man got up and walked away. For 38 years the man had been carried to the pool, but when Jesus spoke only seven words the man was healed in a fraction of a minute. It's wonderful to see the power of the Word.

On another occasion a Roman centurion, considering himself unworthy to approach Jesus, sent Jewish elders to Him that He might come and heal a servant who was desperately ill. This Roman officer loved Israel and had built a synagogue for the Jews. Jesus responded to the call; but before He reached the centurion's home, friends met the Lord with a message of such faith from the centurion that it caused Jesus to say, *"I have not found so great faith, no, not in Israel."* The centurion asked only that Jesus "speak the Word" and his servant would be healed! This man understood authority because he had soldiers under him who obeyed or died. Believing that Jesus' Word had such authority, He entrusted his beloved servant to the power of His Word. What were the results? The servant was healed! (See Luke 7:2-10.)

As a teacher in the Body of Christ, I continually have the privilege of seeing the results of speaking the Word. I want to tell you, it's exciting to see people receive the Word when it is spoken. The Holy Spirit often shows me someone in the congregation who is being changed by the Word. I often feel faith come down in a certain part of a group, and later someone from that area will say they were healed as they responded to the Word which was spoken. It isn't only physical healing that takes place as a result of the spoken Word. I hear testimonies of finances being healed, marriages being healed, and relationships being healed. Anything that needs healing can be healed through the spoken Word.

EARTH'S RESPONSE TO HEAVEN'S ACTION

Next, I want to mention the love and compassion of Jesus to heal. Since I have already discussed this in some detail, I won't spend much time on it here. However, that is not to lessen it's importance. For me, the awareness of God's love is the foundation of everything I can believe or receive. I've said before that everything God has done for us comes out of His great love. Matthew 14:14 says, *"And Jesus went forth, and saw a great multitude, and was moved with compassion toward them, and he healed their sick."*

This incident happened at a time when Jesus had just suffered great personal grief and loss over the murder of John the Baptist. The Lord tried to separate Himself from the crowd; but when they followed Him, He was so touched by their need that He set aside His own need and ministered healing to the people. What a poignant picture of God's love. That same compassion is still at work in hearts and lives. It comes from God and fills His children, causing them to "touch" others with healing power.

Obedience to the Word also brings healing. One day Jesus told a man with a withered arm to stretch out that arm. The man might have exclaimed, "Stretch out my arm; are you a lunatic? I can't stretch out this withered arm." Instead, the man obeyed Jesus' Word; and when he attempted to do as Jesus commanded, the crippled arm was healed (see Matthew 12:13). When Jesus told the man at the pool of Bethesda to get up and walk, that must have sounded preposterous to a man who hadn't walked in 38 years; but he was healed when he tried to stand.

The people in wheelchairs that I see healed made an effort to rise from the chair when a healing Word was spoken to them. It may not even happen immediately, but obedience to the Word brings healing. Sometimes the things God tells you to do may seem strange to your mind, but obedience is the key. What do you suppose the crowd thought when Jesus spit on some dirt, applied it to a blind man's eyes, and told him to go wash off the mud at the pool of Siloam? That man could have missed his healing by getting upset when spitballs were put on his eyes. However, he obeyed the Word and regained his vision.

I get excited over the power of agreement to heal. The

Word tells us that one can chase a thousand, two can chase 10,000, and a threefold cord is not easily broken. Not only does agreement release tremendous power, but it is so encouraging when others stand with you on the Word of God. If you grow faint and discouraged, you need someone else to believe with you. Jesus gave us a wonderful promise in Matthew 18:19 when He said, " . . . *if two of you shall agree on earth as touching any thing that they shall ask, it shall be done for them of my Father which is in heaven."* Even one person praying for another with a healing promise puts two people in agreement, and God is always in agreement with His Word.

Prayer is another God-given tool through which we can receive healing. Prayer is our means of communication with God at all times and in every situation. We don't have to be in church, we don't have to have hands laid on us, we don't have to have someone else agreeing, or be touched by a famous healing evangelist. We can just lift a prayer to the Father, and He hears and answers. He is just a prayer away. James 5:15 tells us, *"And the prayer of faith shall save the sick, and the Lord shall raise him up; and if he have committed sins, they shall be forgiven him."*

One of the finest and most effective missionaries of our day was healed just kneeling in prayer. This man suffered a nervous breakdown; and at the age of 40, he was sent home from the mission field after being given no hope of ministering again. However, in a year he was better; so he went back to India and almost immediately had another collapse. He found a quiet retreat in the mountains but after three months of rest was worse instead of better.

One day in prayer the Lord spoke to this missionary saying, "I want you to win many of the intellectuals of India, because no one is doing this.'' The man was perplexed and he argued with God. At the moment he wasn't capable of doing anything; and if he were, he didn't have the background or training needed to reach the intelligentsia. Then God asked this man if he were willing, and the man said, ''Yes.'' That response brought a healing flow into the man's mind and body, and he was totally restored. This missionary continued to work in India for years, and God used him mightily.

It seems to me that the most powerful way of healing is *faith*. The "faith message" is nothing new in this age; it is as old as God's message to mankind. The words of Hebrews 11:6 are as sure today as they were the day they were written, *"But without faith it is impossible to please him: for he that cometh to God must believe that he is, and that he is a rewarder of them that diligently seek him.''* If God has promised something, He is as good as His Word. *"Listen to me! You can pray for anything, and if you believe, you have it; it's yours!''* (Mark 11:24 TLB).

God has not only promised healing, He has paid for it. Therefore, if we ask and believe, it is ours. One must be sure of God's will and then be diligent in seeking that will. The best way I know to be convinced and diligent is to meditate on the Word of God which speaks specifically to your circumstance. Put the Word in your heart, speak it with your mouth, and it will change your situation; it will remove your sickness. Multitudes of people have removed *"**mountains**"* of difficulty by speaking and speaking and speaking the Word and believing it in their hearts.

Repeatedly Jesus rewarded faith. A hemorrhaging woman, a Roman centurion, friends of a palsied man, several blind people, and the woman who had a demonized daughter received what they needed for themselves or others because of their faith. I could list even more to whom Jesus said, "Your faith has made you whole." However, because of unbelief Jesus healed very few in His own hometown of Nazareth. I know a man who has had a successful healing ministry for half a century. He simply teaches the Word until such a faith level is built in people that they receive their healing. Although this man strongly believes in a miracle-working God, he says he would rather teach faith than work miracles because people can lose what they don't know how to keep.

THE NAME OF JESUS AND A WORD OF DELIVERANCE

Then there is what I call the "quickie" remedy. In Acts 3:1-8 we find Peter and John approaching the Temple by the "Beautiful" gate. Before they made their way through the door, a man who had been crippled from birth begged them for money. This was the cripple's only means of support and every day he was brought to the gate. Money couldn't heal the man, but the disciples had something that could. Peter said, *"Silver and gold have I none; but such as I have give I thee: In the name of Jesus Christ of Nazareth rise up and walk."*

Peter didn't anoint the man with oil; Peter and John didn't lay hands on him; they didn't pray a religious prayer. Peter simply spoke the name of Jesus and commanded the man to rise and walk. Is there power in that name? Indeed there is. The man didn't stumble and gradually get to his feet; he jumped up and began to leap all over the place. The name of Jesus destroyed the lordship of Satan. Listen to Jesus: *"Hitherto have ye asked nothing in my name:*

ask, and ye shall receive, that your joy may be full"
(John 16:24). It was our Lord Himself Who gave us the
authority to use His name. He told believers they would take
lordship over demons and difficult circumstances, they
would lay hands on the sick, and they would recover (see
Mark 16:17,18).

The devil and his demons tremble at the name of Jesus.
Some of Satan's human emissaries arrested Peter and John
and **ordered** them to stop preaching **in that name**. Satan
was furious because thousands were accepting Christ and
the sick were being healed—all in the name of Jesus. When
Peter and John were released, they went to the believers
and called a prayer meeting. Here's what they prayed, *"And
now, Lord, behold their threatenings: and grant unto thy
servants, that with all boldness they may speak thy word,
By stretching forth thine hand to heal: and that signs and
wonders may be done* **by the name of thy holy child
Jesus**.*"* After they prayed, the place where they were was
shaken by the power of God and they were all filled with
the Holy Spirit. Then they went right back to the streets
to preach and heal in Jesus' name. (See Acts 4.)

Just the name of Jesus spared a man from being shot and
killed. I heard this testimony several years ago. The man
was a "big time" gangster when the love of God touched
him and he was born again. He could no longer make a living
in crime, so he started a successful real estate business.
However, the "mob" set out to kill this man. One day a man
bolted into his office, pulled out a gun, and aimed it at the
former gangster. The man had only time to cry, "**Jesus**."
At that name the gun flew out of the assassin's hand, and
he *fell* helpless to the floor. The mob never bothered the
realtor again.

Many times a "word of deliverance" brings healing. The discerning of spirits, one of the gifts of the Holy Spirit listed in I Corinthians 12:10, often operates in delivering the sick. Sometimes you have to speak directly to Satan and the root cause of sickness before healing comes. Jesus rebuked Peter's mother-in-law's fever, and the fever left her. Jesus didn't pray or anoint with oil; He simply spoke a word of deliverance. When the Holy Spirit reveals a root problem of sickness such as a "spirit of infirmity" or a "spirit of death," it can be rebuked and the individual set free from illness and oppression. The Holy Spirit may reveal that bitterness or unforgiveness has brought sickness. When the person is willing to forgive, a word of deliverance will bring healing.

A WORD AND A PRAYER

Another wonderful way in which the Lord ministers healing is through a "word of knowledge." This is mentioned as one of the nine gifts of the Holy Spirit in I Corinthians 12:8. Let me illustrate. As I teach in meetings, the Lord usually gives me a "word of knowledge" about the physical needs of many in the congregation. Not long ago while I was teaching on healing, the Lord let me know there were a number of people there with foot problems. Two notable healings took place when I prayed for those who responded to a call for prayer. One woman had a bone in her foot put back in place, and mobility was restored to a man's foot and ankle which had been fractured several months before. Many others reported that they were instantly relieved of severe pain in their feet. I had no previous knowledge of these foot problems, but the Lord let me in on a bit of His omniscience. Why? Because He loves them and wants to heal them.

The Lord isn't going to let you know things about people just because you are curious or "nosy." God is not a "tattletale," but He will give you information through a "word of knowledge" which enables you to minister or pray more effectively. Believe it or not, He will even give you needed information about yourself. The Lord let me know there was a certain food which was not good for me, so I stopped eating it. At my next physical checkup, the doctor told me I would be wise to avoid the very food which I had already eliminated from my diet. Do you believe the Lord is interested in even the "small" things which concern you? I do!

There are examples in the Scripture where we see a "word of knowledge" in operation. Elisha "knew" that if Naaman dipped in the Jordan River seven times, he would be healed of leprosy. There was nothing supernatural about dipping seven times; neither did the Jordan have any therapeutic powers. Elisha's natural mind would never have proposed such a solution, but it worked because *God* said it would. First Isaiah received "word" that King Hezekiah would be raised from his death bed and live another 15 years. Then they laid a lump of figs on Hezekiah's boil. Wow! Should we all start eating figs or plastering them on our bodies? Of course not. Isaiah had a "word of knowledge" for the king that effected a miraculous cure.

Prayer and fasting is probably the most disciplined method of producing healing. The body is seldom comfortable when deprived of food. Setting aside time to pray when one could be eating requires determination. Nevertheless, the rewards are quite dramatic. Jesus cast a demon out of a child and said, *"This kind goeth not out but by prayer and fasting."*

Matthew 17:14-21 relates the story of a man who brought his epileptic son to Jesus' disciples in order that they might heal him, but they were unable to do so. Jesus rebuked these disciples for their *unbelief*, then He delivered the boy. Notice that Jesus obviously "practiced what He preached"; also notice that prayer combined with fasting *strengthens faith*. Fasting is not a sacrifice which "twists" the arm of God; *fasting subdues our flesh and enables our spirit to hear the voice of God*. Wouldn't you rather live in the Spirit than in the flesh?

I received a triumphant testimony from a woman who had been delivered from a bad situation through fasting and prayer. She had found herself being drawn into a relationship with a married man. The flattering attention she received from him was very satisfying to her flesh, but she was also very frightened. As a Christian this woman knew the relationship was wrong, but no matter how hard she tried she didn't have the strength to break it. When she became desperate, this woman decided to fast and pray about the matter. After three days she was able to walk away from the situation in God's strength. I would say she received *healing* for her soul. It wasn't easy, but God took her yielded will and added His power. That's true will power!

Early in my husband Wally's adult Christian life, a friend of his was admitted to a mental hospital. Wally was so burdened for the man that he decided to do something he had never done before. He fasted—for only one meal, but the Lord graciously honored my husband's obedience and faith. Very shortly Wally heard that his friend had been released from the hospital and was having no more difficulty. Is there someone you know who has an "unshakable" illness; or is there a problem in your own life that has not surrendered to anything you have done? Set aside some time to fast and pray, meditate on the Word, and let your faith level rise to the place of deliverance and healing.

GOD'S PRESENCE HEALS

There is another way of healing that is just dynamite! In Luke 5:17 we read that the very presence of the Lord has power to heal. Jesus was teaching the Pharisees and doctors of the law who had come from everywhere to hear Him, *"and the power of the Lord was present to heal them."* Just how can we enter into the power and the presence of the Lord to receive healing? Psalms 22:3 says, *"But thou art holy, O thou that **inhabitest the praises** of Israel."* Isn't that wonderful! God is so pleased with our praise that He just comes down to fellowship with us, and the holiness of His presence makes sick bodies whole.

The late Kathryn Kuhlman had an unusual healing ministry that was as baffling to her as it was to her audience. She said she didn't know how or why God healed so many in her meetings. The believer and the unbeliever, the skeptic and those full of faith were healed—it didn't seem to matter. However, there was one powerful dynamic in those services. Miss Kuhlman spent hours each day caught up in worshiping and praising the Lord Whom she loved with all her being. When she walked onto a platform, she simply took her audience into that worship and praise; and the power of the Lord was present to heal. Today that "mantle" seems to have fallen on a young pastor who worked in Miss Kuhlman's ministry. This man doesn't spend a long time teaching or preaching in healing services. Instead, he involves the people in praise and worship and healing begins to flow.

Years ago a friend of mine took a real skeptic to one of Miss Kuhlman's meetings. This woman had suffered a severe neck injury in an automobile accident. A fractured bone in her neck had been replaced through surgery, but she still experienced severe pain and some immobility in one arm. That evening the woman became a believer in God's healing power for today when she was healed just sitting there as a spectator. I'm so thankful that Christian woman was willing to swallow her pride and share the good news with my friend. This person has since experienced God's healing touch many times in very critical circumstances.

Another means of healing is the anointing with oil. The anointing with oil was a common practice in the Old Covenant among the Jews. God commanded that kings and priests be anointed with oil, and lepers who were cleansed were anointed with oil. We know that oil signifies the presence of the Holy Spirit. In the New Covenant James writes:

Is any sick among you? let him call for the elders
of the church; and let them pray over him,
anointing him with oil in the name of the Lord:
And the prayer of faith shall save the sick, and
the Lord shall raise him up; . . . (James 5:14,15).

I remember a somewhat amusing incident in my own life which took place when our church was in its infancy. I was suffering from an ear infection which stubbornly resisted medication and prayer. At one point when I was in severe pain, I called my mother for advice. She told me to put a drop or two of warm oil in my ear because that often relieved an earache. Because I didn't have the proper kind of oil in my home, I went to our church, which was not far away, for the bottle of oil with which we anointed members of our congregation when they were sick. I put a few drops of that oil in my ear. Do you know, that was the last of my earache! Then I realized I had used the "anointing" oil in my ear. I don't believe it was any medicinal property in that oil that healed my ear; the oil in that bottle was consecrated for the purpose of anointing the sick. It had been used numerous times to heal other sick bodies, and that day it healed my sick body.

Lastly, I want to mention the sovereign work of God. We simply can't put a formula on every person's healing. Some people are healed, and we just don't know what it was that brought about their healing. We only know that God healed them. Do you understand why the dead soldier who was thrown into the sepulcher containing Elisha's bones was raised to life? Yes, it seems that God's power, which was upon Elisha, still resided in those bones. However, no one expected the soldier to be revived, certainly not the soldier. Prayer wasn't offered for him, hands weren't laid on him, and no one anointed him with oil. Nevertheless, God raised that soldier from the dead. I believe he was a God-fearing man after that, don't you?

People traveling to Miss Kuhlman's meetings were healed on the buses, and others were healed walking into the auditoriums where the meetings were held. If I tried to come up with an answer or a formula for every healing, I would only be guessing. I don't have all the answers, and neither do you; but this one thing I do know, *God loves people.* He wants to make them well and whole in every way, and He will go to any means possible to manifest His loving grace in our lives. Let's use all the ways the Lord has given us to heal and be healed. Speak the Word, send the Word, believe the Word, anoint with oil, use Jesus' name, rebuke sickness, fast and pray— use it all. Live expectantly, and trust God to use His unlimited power and resources on your behalf at your request!

Chapter Five
THE HEART MENDER

It was impossible, but I was seeing it with my own eyes. The picture of the two men, arm-in-arm, moved my heart in an unspeakable way. These two men were worlds apart, and yet a gesture of love had brought them together. I'm always surprised when a news magazine reports good news, but this story was obviously newsworthy. I want to tell you the story behind that picture which involved a Jewish cantor and a *former* Ku Klux Klan member. It all began when the Klansman started sending filthy, evil notes to the cantor and also leaving his sick messages on the cantor's answering machine because he was eaten up with hatred for all Jewish people.

Angry and frustrated, the Jewish man called the police to see if they had an answer to his dilemma. Although the man thought he knew who might be doing these terrible things, he couldn't prove it; and the law enforcement people could offer no solution. Then the Jewish man took the matter into his own hands; he started putting messages on the Klansman's phone. However, these messages had a different tone to them. The cantor told the Klansman that if he had lived in Nazi Germany when the Jews were being exterminated, he would have been exterminated right along with them because he was a cripple. The Nazis, in attempting to produce the "super race," had killed all those who were handicapped mentally or physically. With just short phone messages, the Jewish man made an attempt to inform the "hater" that he was involved in something that was both cruel and inhuman.

Eventually one evening the angry Klansman called the Jewish cantor and asked why he was putting the messages on his phone. Why indeed! With as much kindness as possible the cantor explained to the other man that he was caught in an awful lie and his heart was all wrong. "You are in something very evil that is going to destroy you," the cantor said. He concluded the conversation by expressing concern over how the crippled man did his grocery shopping, and the cantor asked if he and his wife could do the Klansman's grocery shopping that week. However, the Klansman refused the offer.

After a few more weeks and a few more kind messages, the Jewish man called and asked if his wife could prepare a meal to bring to the crippled man. This time he said, "Yes." However, before the cantor and his wife took over the meal, the wife expressed a desire to buy the man a silver ring. They purchased the ring and took the lovely gift along with the meal. After eating together, the Jewish couple presented the man with the beautifully wrapped gift. Overwhelmed by the couple's love and generosity, the Klansman viewed the contents of the small box, then removed from his finger a ring engraved with a German swastika and placed the new ring on his finger.

Today that former Ku Klux Klan member has renounced the organization and travels our nation speaking to young people about the terrible dangers of hate groups and the lies that put hate in people's hearts against others. This man's life was totally turned around by the love of someone he hated, and today the two men are the best of friends. When asked by the press to give an explanation to what had happened, the Jewish cantor replied, "My Jewish faith teaches that you should be kind to your enemies, so I decided to practice what I preached—and it worked!" This gracious Jewish man and his wife may not know Jesus as their Messiah; but they practiced what the Word teaches, and the Word always works.

YOUR HEART IS A TREASURY

Did you know that healing really begins in the heart? Healing works from the inside out. Jesus announced to a hurting, dying world that He was anointed by the life-giving Spirit of God to preach good news to the poor. All of us are poor and lacking unless there is a dynamic flow of God's Spirit in our lives. Jesus went right to the "heart" of the matter when, first of all, He said He came to *heal the brokenhearted.* Why must healing power begin in the heart? Proverbs 4:23 gives the answer, "*Keep thy heart with all diligence; for out of it are the issues of life.*" Out of your innermost being comes the response to any situation with which you will ever deal. Your tongue is "attached" to the contents of your heart; as you draw out those contents with your tongue, you guide yourself toward life or death:

> . . . *for out of the abundance of the heart the mouth speaketh. A good man out of the good treasure of the heart bringeth forth good things: and an evil man out of the evil treasure bringeth forth evil things* (Matthew 12:34,35).

That truth is awesome and attention getting. If you are a good person, it is only because you have been storing good things in the treasury of your heart. What makes an evil person? The evil things which are stored in the heart. Jesus came to preach and teach good news; He Himself is the Word and what He taught was good. Jesus, the Word, is our heart mender. His Word stored in our hearts will heal and transform our hearts and our lives. One day Jesus asked a man why he called Him good. Jesus explained that only God is good. Our Lord was telling the man that He was God, and He was good. When God and His Word live in the heart, the heart can be mended and healed.

Every person in the world has had ample opportunity to store "evil" things in their hearts. You've probably heard the expression, "Life doesn't deal from a straight deck." In other words, life isn't fair; it is stacked with all manner of disappointments, failures, lies, misconceptions, and catastrophes of every sort. All these things stored in the heart produce heartache. The Lord Jesus came to remove the heartache and bring wholeness to our hearts. Praise the Lord! He has the ability to pluck the junk out of your heart and remove the heartache; He will remove the poverty of your heart and soul and bestow His riches there. Then you must fill your heart with the exceeding great and precious promises of God which II Peter 1:3,4 says will provide *everything* you need for life and godliness.

Our newspaper recently carried a tragic article concerning a man who gave his mother a gun with which to kill herself. The man was on trial for being instrumental in his mother's death. Why did this man do such a horrible thing? Why did his mother kill herself? Because they both believed a lie. This son *thought* he was doing a loving, merciful thing— because he had believed a lie. The mother had been having some physical problems and medical tests indicated there was cancer in her body. So without waiting for further tests, this poor woman, who was unwilling to suffer and die with cancer, took her own life with the gun provided by her son. After her death, it was learned that there had been no cancer in the mother's body. Her son was acquitted, but how severely he must have judged himself. I shudder when I think of the grief and the guilt with which this man must be dealing. How he needs Jesus' love and forgiveness to heal his broken heart.

How many are sick and die early because they believe the lies of the devil? You know, it's like putting a gun to your head and shooting yourself. Satan is a liar and the father of every lie; his purpose is to plant lies in every human heart, especially lies about God. He hopes that you will "buy" into his lies and never be changed by God's truth and His love. If your heart is wrong it is difficult to receive healing for your physical body. Bitterness, resentment, envy, unforgiveness, and guilt, all this kind of junk and garbage from hell keeps people from the ability to receive healing. These things will cause anyone to hold back from God or to feel guilty before Him. Then healing can't really flow because the heart is full of other things. Instead, we need to believe Truth; God says He loves us and desires to give us a long and happy life.

Love never fails. Let me say it again; love never fails! A hair stylist, who attends our church, told me this amazing story of God's love. One evening he came home from work and found his front door unlocked. Knowing that he never left the door unlocked and feeling that someone was in the apartment, he cautiously searched the rooms. When the man entered the bathroom, there was a man trying to hide in the bathtub. The intruder was a large man, capable of overpowering my friend. However, a peace enveloped my friend and very calmly he asked, "What are you doing in my apartment?"

The man in the tub replied that someone had been breaking into apartments on that floor, and he had chased the individual into that apartment. When he didn't find the burglar, he decided to stay and protect the apartment—in the bathtub.

Telling the man how very kind that was, my friend suggested they both go look for the burglar. After ushering him into the hall, he said they really should tell the manager, so together they went to the manager's office. The cosmetologist said to the manager, "I found this man in my apartment; he says he was looking for a burglar, but I think *he* is the burglar." The man admitted it was true; he was the burglar. Praise the Lord, the man was caught before anything was taken, and no one was hurt. My friend told me that he had a gun in the apartment; but when he thought about getting it, the Lord spoke to him and said, "Don't use the gun; use your *love!*"

A person may easily accept the fact that God is love, but that fact can be very intimidating when we realize that God expects us to love as He loves. That may not be so easy. I can just hear someone saying, "Of course, God can love; He's God, but I'm not like that." Now wait a minute! In Whose image and in Whose likeness are we all created? If we are made in God's image, who do we think we are like? He didn't make us like the devil; He made us like Himself. We see God's image in Jesus Christ; and when Jesus lives in our hearts we **can** love as He loves. You and I were cut out of God material, so we bear the mark or stamp of God's love— the love that *can* love and *wants* to love. Don't get the "can'ts"; get the "cans."

WE HAVE A PRIMARY AND A SECONDARY NATURE

We have a primary nature—the nature mankind was first given by God, the love nature. God said that nature was good because it was like Him. However, when Adam and Eve sinned, they opened the door to a secondary nature which is not good. That secondary nature is a nature of sin and a nature of hate. So we have a primary nature and a secondary nature, and the two are opposed to one another. Before you accepted Christ, you knew that love could warm your heart, you enjoyed loving others, and it felt good to be loved. You were responding to your primary nature— God's stamp on your being—even though you weren't born again. It didn't feel good to sin or to hate because God didn't make you that way.

People say it's just our nature to sin, so we can't keep from sinning. Yes, we have a sin nature, and all it can do is sin; but that isn't the nature God gave us—it is a secondary nature. The fact that sin will destroy your life proves that we weren't made to handle sin. Sin will make you uncomfortable, and it will make you feel guilty because it's not like your primary nature. There's not one part of us that can cope with sin: not our spirits, not our minds, not our emotions, and not our bodies. Sin may bring pleasure for a little while, but in the end it will destroy. (See Hebrews 11:25.) Romans 6:23 makes it clear that the wages of sin is death. God made us for life and love. Love does not destroy; it builds and heals. Love sustains and protects us.

Paul so ably described the warfare of the two natures within us when he wrote Romans 7:19-25. Who would know better the nature of hate and the nature of love? Paul was a murderer who became one of the greatest missionaries of love the world has ever known. Listen to Paul:

> *For the good that I would I do not: but the evil which I would not, that I do. Now if I do that I would not, it is no more I that do it, but sin that dwelleth in me. I find then a law, that, when I*

*would do good, evil is present with me. For **I delight in the law of God after the inward man**: But I see another law in my members, warring against the law of my mind, and bringing me into captivity to the law of sin which is in my members.*

Paul cried out to know how he could be delivered of the warfare in his soul: *"O wretched man that I am! who shall deliver me from the body of this death?"* But Paul had found the answer to his own question, and he answered it for you and for me when he said, *"I thank God through Jesus Christ our Lord. So then with the mind I myself serve the law of God; but with the flesh the law of sin."* Paul knew by experience that the power of sin is broken and the guilt and condemnation of sin is removed from those who walk after the spirit and not after the flesh. (See Romans 8:1.)

When we receive Jesus, our first nature lines up with the nature of God and it has the power in Christ to subdue the second nature. There is a law that comes into you and me when we are reborn that sets us free from the secondary nature. That law of the Spirit of life in Christ will set you free from sin and death because you have Christ in you. (See Romans 8:2.) He is your hope of living out of your primary nature, your expectation of walking in all God's goodness and glory. (See Colossians 1:27.) In Christ we can lay hold of that hope which is a sure and steadfast anchor of the soul according to Hebrews 6:18,19. Jesus Christ, our Hope, will take us into the very presence of God.

We all know that we become like those with whom we associate, so let's all take advantage of associating with Father God and His Son, Jesus Christ. Hear the words of I John 1:3 and 3:1-3:

. . . truly our fellowship is with the Father, and with his Son Jesus Christ. Behold, what manner of love the Father hath bestowed upon us, that we should be called the sons of God: . . . Beloved, **now are we the sons of God,** *and it doth not yet appear what we shall be: but we know that, when he shall appear, we shall be like him; for we shall see him as he is. And* **every man that hath this hope in him purifieth himself, even as he is pure.**

The apostle John wrote more about God's love and the operation of His love in us than any other writer of the Scriptures. John was called the "beloved" apostle; he was a man who flowed in God's love because he knew and understood the love of God. However, John had not always been such a man. Before John yielded totally to God's love, he often expressed his secondary nature. Jesus named John and his brother James "sons of thunder," and once John wanted Jesus to call fire down on some people. The Lord told John that he wasn't aware of the spirit (nature) from which that wrong attitude came. Love transformed John; and with the insight of the Holy Spirit, he wrote, *"We love him, because he first loved us"* (I John 4:19.)

You didn't love God first; He loved you first. You may think you were looking for God, but all the time He was pursuing you, watching over you because His desire was to pour out His love upon you. You responded to His love and began to love Him back. Without receiving *His* kind of love, you could never have truly loved Him. Religions teach you to climb to God by doing good deeds, afflicting the body, or abiding by their rules and regulations; but no one can climb to God. Instead, Jesus is THE "ladder" which God sent down to us, His ladder of love.

Even many Christian groups put so much stress on "doing" that their membership works and works to please God. They count the Bible chapters they read, the hours they pray, and the meetings they attend. They fast and deny the flesh—always hoping to do enough to stay in God's "good graces," but never finding the liberty of God's grace which sets us free from works. Because His love has touched us, we love to fellowship with Him in the Word and prayer, to fellowship with other believers, to walk in the Spirit—*we love God*. There is such exhilarating freedom in His love!

The opportunity to speak at a Mormon women's retreat was one of the most unusual I've ever received. One woman in the group became born again and "spearheaded" the invitation. After a few sessions some of the women challenged me for talking as though an individual could know they were saved. According to their doctrine, that information will only be available when Jesus comes because salvation is dependent upon works; the greater your works, the higher your heaven. These precious, sincere women were all trying to climb to heaven on a ladder of works. It's just the opposite! We don't go up the ladder; He comes down the ladder to the lowest rung where we are, stretches out His arms and says, "I love you exactly as you are."

Hang onto your hats. I have a marvelous praise report from the retreat! I was told that at no time could I give an invitation to receive salvation, but God gave me different instructions. Before the last meeting, the Lord said, "I want you to go in there and offer salvation to those women." I reminded the Lord about what I had been told; but He didn't change His mind. He reminded me that it was the last meeting, so what could they do; I was packing up and leaving town anyway. Ah ha, I found that God is smarter than I am. So I went into that last session, presented the plan of salvation, and the hand of every woman in the room went up to receive Jesus. That is, every hand but one. That hand belonged to the born-again woman who had invited me.

FOUR BASIC ASPECTS OF GOD'S LOVE

God's love is a unique kind of love which is absolutely unconditional; it expects nothing in return from the person who is loved. I'm not saying that love may not be returned, but God's love is not prompted by what it can receive. "Agape" is the word used for the God kind of love. When you receive Jesus and experience "agape" love, that same "agape" love resides in you because you are one with Him. Romans 5:5 says: " . . . *the love of God is shed abroad in our hearts by the Holy Ghost* . . . ." The love that fills your heart is no different than God's "agape" love. Therefore, you have the potential to love just exactly the way God loves.

I'm going to describe four basic aspects of "agape" love. First, it is *spontaneous* and *unmotivated*. God doesn't look down from His heavenly throne and pick out a good prospect to love. He isn't looking for high I.Q., a great physique, outstanding ability, charming personality, etc. No, every one of us is loved *spontaneously* by God. He doesn't wait to see if we are going to "turn out" good or bad, tall or short, rich or poor. God never looks for our potential before He will love us. There are simply no conditions we have to meet in order to be loved by God. All we have to do is step into His love; the door is marked "Jesus."

The second marvelous thing about God's love is that it is indifferent to value received. You know, we tend to like people who can give us something. They may be able to help us, or promote us, get us into the right places, or do a wonderful thing for us. So we love them for what we can get out of the deal. These people we choose have something to give us in return for our love. That isn't the way God loves. What could we possibly give God in return for His love? I imagine God thinking, "I'm not going to get anything out of this, but I will love anyway. I can't help loving, because I am love." He loves the righteous as well as the unrighteous, and He sends the rain on the just and the unjust. (See Matthew 5:45.) Why? Because His nature is love, and "agape" love always seeks to give, not to get.

I read this week about a woman whose life was spared because of "agape" love. One night this lady walked into her London apartment and discovered a robber helping himself to her valuables. Right then the man could have killed her. Who knows the fear that might have gripped her heart? However, instead of fear there was something much better in her heart; it was the "agape" love of God which expects nothing in return. Instead of screaming, the lady said, "You have broken into my apartment and you are taking the most precious things I have; evidently you must need them more than I do, so you may have them. I give them to you, so you don't have to steal them." Then the woman led the robber to where she had other valuables hidden and showed them to him. This totally unnerved the thief who said, "Lady, I can't handle this"; and he turned and walked out leaving everything behind including his gun.

Perhaps the most inspiring and awesome thing about God's love is that it is creative. It doesn't look for something of value, but it takes *nothing* and creates *something* of great value. Isn't that wonderful? We might look at somebody and see nothing worthwhile; but with a look of love, God sees a vessel of infinite value. Then He begins His creative work. Recently I called a pastor whom I didn't know concerning a missions project. We chatted awhile and he told me he had been a youth pastor in a church where I had held a Bible Encounter. Then I remembered this pastor's testimony.

When this man was 17 years old, he and a friend got high on drugs, murdered a woman, and cut her up with a butcher knife. I know that's horrible, but just wait. The young man went to prison, and his mother and father went every weekend to see him. The mother, who was a Christian, prayed continually for her son who was unsaved, a murderer, and whose life was in shambles. Then a Christian music group came to the prison, and this murderer was saved. A few weeks later he was filled with the Holy Spirit. He was so changed by the love of God that he soon became the prison chaplain.

Seven years later this man was among seven murderers chosen by the state attorney to be released because of their model behavior. Well, that was unheard of! His parents worried about what freedom would do to him; but after going home, he enrolled in Bible school. After graduation he became the youth pastor in the church where he had seen me. Later he married a fine Christian girl and took the pastorate where he is now. The story just gets better and better. Because he had been on drugs for several years, he supposed he couldn't father any children. His wife recently presented him with triplets! Just see what God's creative love can do. As the expression says, "God doesn't make junk." He sees everyone as a diamond in the rough. Only the touch of the Master is needed to create a sparkling gem of exquisite beauty.

Lastly, God's love initiates fellowship with Him. We were lost and undone in this world, without hope and estranged from God until His love touched us and brought us into the family. Now we can have continual fellowship with the Father and our elder brother Jesus Christ. (See Ephesians 2:12,13.) You love to be around someone who loves you, don't you? You just feel so comfortable with them and you enjoy their fellowship. The love God has for us causes us to desire His fellowship too. I delight in God's presence and in His fellowship. I know He is my friend:

> *According as he hath chosen us in him before the foundation of the world, that we should be holy and without blame before him in love: Having predestinated us unto the adoption of children by Jesus Christ to himself, according to the good pleasure of his will, To the praise of the glory of his grace, wherein he hath made us accepted in the beloved* (Ephesians 1:4-6).

I don't enjoy being around a person who never compliments me, who never has a good word for me, a person who is always picking at me or criticizing the way I do things. You don't either. There is no real fellowship with a person like that. However, when we have full assurance of someone's love, we can receive constructive criticism and feel built up rather than torn down. It's the same with God. Even when He corrects us, it's so sweet because we know it comes out of His love. God's loving correction keeps us on course, and keeps us from making mistakes. We would miss all that if we weren't in fellowship with a God Who loves us and cares about what happens to us. First John 1:7 says that when we walk in the light as God is in the light, we have fellowship with Him and with one another.

LOVE YOURSELF AND OTHERS WITH GOD'S LOVE

Does God expect us to love ourselves? We are able to give love back to God because He planted His love in our hearts, but what about loving ourselves? That is often the hardest thing in the world to do, but the Lord tells us to love others *as we love ourselves.* (See Matthew 19:19.) I have counted nine times in the New Testament where the love we are commanded to have for others is based on the love we have for ourselves. We are usually harder on ourselves than anyone else. If you go around hating or disliking yourself, in spite of God's love for you, you're out of the will of God. Are you going to love what God loves and hate what God hates? Well, *God loves you,* so love yourself.

Since we have the "agape" love of God in us which enables us to love Him, we can also love ourselves with "agape" love. That doesn't mean that you will always be pleased with yourself or ignore the mistakes you make because you are so extra special to you. It doesn't mean that you can run "rough shod" over other people. That is selfishness, not love. Let's look again at the four attributes of God's love, and then we will learn how we can properly and constructively love ourselves.

First, your love must be unconditional and unmotivated. You can't love yourself when you are "good" and then hate yourself when you are "bad." Love for self is not based on achievement or the value others place on you. You must love yourself even when you stick your feet in the drawer and waste an entire day, or when you stick your foot in your mouth and embarrass everyone including yourself. Loving yourself with God's love creates something in you that gives you a good image. You see, God loves you exactly as you are right now. He sees every fault and every asset, but none of these things alter God's love for you in any way.

God's love brings immeasurable security to our lives. It enables us to be secure about ourselves. This kind of security enables you to correct your mistakes without self condemnation, and to regard your achievements without pride. When you "blow it," repent and always remember you're in the making for something better, *"For it is God which worketh in you both to will and to do of his good pleasure* (Philippians 2:13). The way to satisfaction, success, and creative fulfillment is by placing the same value on your life that God does. Proper appreciation for self will cause you to enjoy your own company; even **others** will enjoy your company, but your best fellowship will be with the Lord. "Agape" love for self brings contentment to the heart, rewarding friendships with others, and satisfying, refreshing fellowship with God.

Now that you love yourself, you can love anyone else as God loves them. Does that sound like an impossible assignment? Not when you love others with "agape" love. That same love of God, with which you love Him and love yourself, is the same love with which you can love others. God's love resides within you, and it doesn't take a vacation when you encounter someone you "just can't stand." Remember, "agape" love is unconditional. It isn't enough just to love your friends, you must love your enemies. That's "agape." Jesus said that even the heathen can love their own friends, but the mark of a believer is found in the love he has for his enemies. Ouch!

It's easy to love people who dress like we do, enjoy the same kind of movies, like the same restaurants, share the same opinions, and have similar backgrounds or education. We relate to these kinds of people, don't we? However, God's love in us will love spontaneously and will have no self-serving motivation. Allow yourself to see others through the Lord's eyes, and you will "fall in love" with people. When you love as God loves, you will be indifferent to value. Your love will not be determined by whether or not an individual can be of value to you. How freeing it is to find something you can do for others instead of looking for something they can do for you. You will never come out on the short end. God will repay all your kindness and love.

It is so exciting to know that I can create something worthwhile in another person just by loving and encouraging them. A young man, who is now an employee of our church, attended our Christian school and played basketball on the school team. The other day he told my husband Wally a story that brought a smile to my face. He told Wally that every time he was up for a free throw, I would yell at the top of my lungs, "Come on, you can do it, you're good, you're good!" He didn't think he was really good; but he thought, "I'd better be good, because Marilyn is expecting me to be good." You know what? He would always do better than he thought he could. How important is a free throw? Well, how important is it to build confidence in an individual? The young man has never forgotten that, and I believe he is a better achiever today because I encouraged him to be.

God's love for others builds bridges over which we can walk into wonderful fellowship. When you love with God's love, it's easy to have fellowship. In a real relationship, you don't major on differences even though there will always be differences; no two individuals are alike. In true fellowship, people always find something to enjoy about one another; they enjoy conversation or simply the presence of that other individual. Did you ever meet someone you didn't know, but when the two of you discovered you were both Christians, there was instant fellowship? There was instant communication as the love of God flowed between you.

I have a great example from a lady who called our prayer line to share a wonderful praise report. This lady frequently walked to a park near her home and enjoyed sitting there on a bench. She and another woman, who were only "park-bench acquaintances," started visiting with one another. One day the lady disclosed to her "friend" that a large growth had been found in her abdomen. Immediately the other woman prayed for her, and God performed a miracle. The lady felt pain and movement in her abdomen, and after examination she could no longer feel the growth. It had disappeared! Why did the lady call *our* prayer line with this good report? Because the woman who prayed for her attends our church. Praise the Lord, we are "creating" agape lovers!

There are four things which love does: it forgives, it covers sin, it heals, and it creates. I want to examine the lives of three people who made love their major theme when they wrote the Word of God. One of these men is Peter, who began his walk with Jesus as a headstrong, uneducated fisherman. Nevertheless, Jesus hung in with this man because He loved Peter with unconditional love. The devil tried to "sift Peter like wheat," but Jesus prayed for him. Peter's denial of Christ seemed evidence enough that he didn't really love Jesus; but Jesus came to Peter with His love and asked, "Peter, do you love me?" Peter realized he couldn't love Jesus with his own love; he ran out of it. Only God's love, which was shed abroad in Peter's heart by the Holy Spirit, could stand the test. Peter learned to draw on that love, and in I Peter 4:8 he wrote that love covers a multitude of sins. Peter had learned this by experience.

Love created a "new" man out of Peter, and then Peter created another with that love. It was a young man named John Mark. When Paul refused to take John Mark on any more missionary journeys, Peter took him "under his wing." John Mark had been with Paul on a missions' trip to Pamphylia, but the young man quit and went home to Mama. That was enough for Paul, but Peter worked with John Mark and made him his "spiritual" son. This loving encouragement created a man whom the Holy Spirit could use to write the gospel of Mark. Although Mark was not one of the disciples who walked with Jesus, Peter imparted to him all the information necessary to write the gospel. Can't you just see Mark listening with rapt attention as the older man lovingly shared his experiences with the Lord?

Now, let's take a look at John. Everybody thinks John, "the beloved apostle," is so sweet; but he wasn't sweet when he started. Remember I told you Jesus called him a "son of thunder" because of his temper. John and his brother James wanted to destroy some Samaritans with fire. Their mother was brash enough to ask Jesus if they could sit in major places of authority on either side of Christ when He came into His kingdom. John was the kind who would have shoved people out of line at the supermarket. What transformed this man? It was the love with which Jesus loved him. You can't rub elbows with love without that love rubbing off on you.

This same man later went to the Samaritans whom he had wanted to burn up, and he and Peter prayed with them to receive the baptism with the Holy Spirit. (See Acts 8:14,15.) Love changed a man who had murder in his heart into a man who just wanted to share and minister the love of God. Jesus created "agape" love in John's heart, and John turned around and created that same love in others. John loved Jesus so much that he always stayed close to him. He gained an unusual understanding of God's love, and he wrote more clearly about love in one gospel and three small epistles than most any other writer of scripture. Today God's love is still creating and changing the lives of those who take John's writing to heart.

The third man who was dramatically changed by the creative power of God's love is Paul. It was Paul who held the coats of those who stoned Stephen, giving assent to his murder. That's not all! Paul was such a zealous Jew that he traveled hundreds of miles, even across national boundaries, to arrest members of the heretical "sect" of Christians. Then these Christians were often murdered for their faith. Today we would describe Paul as a mass murderer, and yet Jesus loved this hateful man so much that He personally appeared to Paul after the Resurrection and Ascension and turned him around in the direction of love. The encounter with God's love healed Paul's heart and created a totally new man.

Talk about a changed man! Paul said he loved his fellow Jews so much that, if it were possible, he would give up his own salvation to win their salvation. If that isn't the God kind of love, I don't know what is. Who would give up their own salvation and give it to another? Paul expressed a willingness to spend eternity in hell for the sake of men who were trying to murder him. First Corinthians 13, the "love chapter" of the Bible, was written by Paul. What a revelation it is of God's love for us, as well as His love working through us. No one knew better than Paul the creative miracle of God's love.

SURRENDER TO GOD'S LOVE WILL CONQUER FEAR

If we are going to walk in the fullness of God's love, then we need to know what can hinder that love from working in our lives. First John 4:18 says, *"There is no fear in love; but perfect love casteth out fear: because fear hath torment. He that feareth is not made perfect in love."*

What keeps us from being loving? What keeps our hearts all upset? It's **fear**! Fear comes, bringing torment with it, when we are not secure in God's love. If we are not really sure God loves us or if we think we aren't good enough for Him to love, then we open ourselves to fear. Have you heard the warning against "taking your life into your own hands"? That is exactly what we do when insecurity and fear cause us to doubt God's ability to profitably guide our lives. When we take our lives in our own hands, we will make all kinds of mistakes which reinforce our fears.

How do we get rid of fear? Jesus is once again our best example. In John 12:27 Jesus said, *"Now is my soul **troubled**; and what shall I say? Father, save me from this hour: but for this cause came I unto this hour."* What caused Jesus to be troubled? Certain Greeks had come to worship at Jerusalem, and they asked to see Jesus. When Andrew and Philip conveyed this message, the Lord said, "The hour is come that the Son of man should be glorified." Then He told them He was destined to die. I believe the Greeks would have changed that destiny by taking Jesus to Greece and making Him a great philosopher in a culture that held wisdom and learning in the highest esteem. Jesus was being tempted to leave Jerusalem, and the Jews persecuting Him were already looking for a reason to crucify Him.

We know that as a man Jesus shrank from the Cross; it was a fearful thing to face. In Gethsemane Jesus was so troubled that He sweat drops of blood. What caused Jesus to fear? It was the Cross. Jesus struggled in great agony when faced with the Cross. He knew He could walk away from it all—and leave you and me behind. However, Jesus conquered the fear that tried to grip Him and **surrendered** to the Father's will. He said, " . . . *not my will, but thine, be done"* (Luke 22:42). How was Jesus able to face the Cross? He surrendered to the Father because He knew the Father's will was best. Again, on the Cross, Jesus was troubled and fearful when He cried, " . . . *My God, my God, why hast thou forsaken me?"* (Matthew 27:46). However, Jesus' last utterance from the Cross was one of surrender when He released His spirit into His Father's hands.

Paul was so surrendered to the will of God that when he wrote from a Roman jail he could say:

> . . . *the things which happened unto me have fallen out rather unto the furtherance of the gospel; So that my bonds in Christ are manifest in all the palace, and in all other places; And many of the brethren in the Lord, waxing confident by my bonds, are much more bold to speak the word without fear* (Philippians 1:12-14).

Paul wasn't afraid of being in prison because it caused other Christians to lose their fear and to preach boldly the Word of God. In prison Paul was able to win many in Caesar's palace to Christ. Of course, we know that it was while Paul was imprisoned that he wrote 13 epistles which comprise a major portion of the New Testament. He wasn't out preaching the gospel, but those letters have reached millions of people.

Paul was no stranger to the inside of a jail, but it didn't disturb his peace. Once when he was beaten and thrown into jail, Paul was still singing praises to the Lord at midnight. This man wasn't whining and pining because he knew God would work out everything for his good. God was so pleased that He opened the prison doors with an earthquake; but Paul didn't leave. Instead he stayed and led the jailer to Jesus. The jailer got his family, and the whole bunch were saved. Paul never looked for comfort; he looked for results. Men could throw Paul into prison, but they couldn't throw him into fear because he was secure in God's love. It was Paul who wrote these words in Romans 8:28, *"And we know that all things work together for good to them that love God, to them who are the called according to his purpose."*

What did Jesus do? What did Paul do? They surrendered to God! I believe any area of our lives that is not surrendered to the Lord will keep us in fear! We don't always realize our fears, but do you believe God loves you? Do you think He is big enough to take care of you? If you do, you can totally surrender to the Lord; and all fear, known and unknown, will then be in God's hands. When you are surrendered to God, He is able to take care of any trial you face, no matter how big it looks to you. Maybe all you can do is be willing to surrender. God will accept that and strengthen your will. Do you realize to what you are surrendering? You are surrendering to God's love. Remember John's words, *"There is no fear in love; but perfect love casteth out fear: . . . "* (I John 4:18). If you know Jesus, His perfect love is in your heart. It's God's supernatural "agape" love which heals the broken heart. Jesus is your heart mender!

Chapter Six
LIFE UNDER THE SON

Do you like popcorn? Yes or no, you will just love the kind of popcorn I'm going to serve you now! This popcorn is far better than Cracker Jacks or cheese corn; it's "testimony" corn. I'm just going to serve you some "popcorn" testimonies of a few dynamic and wonderful healings which have taken place in our Encounters. One of the most unique miracles of healing took place not long after the Lord began to confirm the Word, which I was teaching, with signs following:

> *And they went forth, and preached every where,*
> *the Lord working with them, and confirming the*
> *word with signs following* (Mark 16:20).

One evening during a service, I was just praying a general prayer for healing. I didn't have people stand, nor were hands laid on anyone, but God moved. After the prayer a woman and her daughter testified that both of them had a "necklace" of small warts instantly removed from around their necks. It was an inherited problem which afflicted other women in the family also. You see, God is so loving that even the "smallest" things are not overlooked by Him. Don't ever think your problem is too small for our great big God.

A more dramatic healing occurred when a small child, who had never heard a sound, received her hearing. This little girl wasn't even in the service, but her mother was anointed with oil in proxy for the child who was in the church nursery. This precious mother had come with faith in her heart for her two year old. A while later everyone's attention was drawn to the rear of the auditorium when a *very* excited woman rushed through the door. It was the mother of the deaf child. After prayer she had slipped out and gone to the nursery to check her little girl. She was overwhelmed with joy when she found that God had opened both the child's ears. The pastor of the church knew the woman and her child, so he verified the healing. A wave of praise and thanksgiving swept through the congregation when the child was brought to the front and we proved she could hear perfectly!

Here's another testimony concerning a six-year-old boy who was having as many as six severe nose bleeds a day. After prayer the boy was healed of this terrible hemorrhaging which was draining away his very life. Nothing had been able to stop it—but God did! A year later the mother reported that her son had not had one nose bleed after we prayed. I remember a woman who had two lumps in her breast, one on her arm, and two on her neck. After prayer they disappeared—lumps, bumps, and all!

In another service a woman's knee was healed. After three surgeries the knee was still popping and giving the lady extreme pain. Her knee was healed during the anointing service, and the delighted lady began to run up and down the aisles. Now that's a good "popcorn" testimony, isn't it? It's much better than popping knees! Has my special bowl of "popcorn" strengthened your faith for healing? That is exactly what I want it to do. The same healing power of God which touched these people is able to touch you or someone you love.

LIFE UNDER THE SUN OR LIFE UNDER THE SON

Everyone under the sun is subject to all kinds of afflictions and ailments, but all these things have to melt away when we live in the light of the S-O-N. That is God's Son, the Lord Jesus Christ! I want to show you some exciting truth from a very philosophical book in the Bible, the book of Ecclesiastes. I used to have trouble enjoying this portion of the Scriptures because it seemed to be just a book of moans and groans. I called it the "book of old groans." The writer was always saying, "Vanity, vanity, all is vanity." I thought the message was hopeless and depressing—until the Holy Spirit revealed to me what was really being said here. Wow, what an exciting book it became!

Solomon, the author of Ecclesiastes, kept using the phrase, "Life under the sun"; but I want you to compare with me "life under the s-u-n" to "life under the S-o-n." What a difference! It took the wisest man who ever lived a long time to get back to this truth after he had left the light of God's wisdom and satisfaction to seek the wisdom and pleasure of the world. And what did Solomon find in life under the sun? Trying to prove to himself that the world's way was better, this "wisest" of all men found only *vanity*. His search was all in vain:

> *Who among you is wise or clever? Let his right conduct give practical proof of it, with the modesty that comes of wisdom. But if you are harboring bitter jealousy and* **selfish ambition** *in your hearts, consider whether your claims are not false, and a defiance of the truth. This is not the wisdom that comes from above; it is earthbound, sensual, demonic. . . . But the wisdom from above is in the first place pure; and then peace-loving, considerate, and open to reason; it is straightforward and sincere, rich in mercy and in the kindly deeds that are its fruit* (James 3:13-17 NEB).

King Solomon was no different than the rest of us. What can we expect living **under** the circumstances of life? If you listen to all the advertisements on TV and read what is in the newspaper, you can expect to feel badly or to be overtaken by some sort of evil. Most all of the products advertised are to make you well because you are sick, make you clean because you are dirty, make you smell good because you stink—or satisfy every lustful desire of your flesh. That is *life under the sun.* Solomon advised us to remember the Creator while we are young, before the evil days come and the years draw nigh when we find no pleasure in life (see Ecclesiastes 12:1).

What is Solomon saying? He is saying we had better remember God while we are young, because when we get older our bodies will wear out and our minds will be so clouded that we can't enjoy God or life anymore. Solomon then paints a word picture of what is going to happen to an aging body. In allegorical fashion, he describes feet as "keepers of the house," knees as "strong men," teeth as "grinders," and eyes and ears as "windows" and "doors." Solomon says old feet are going to tremble and old knees are going to bow, so that a person can no longer stand or walk without difficulty. In other words, the body will become feeble. Solomon says the aged are going to lose their teeth, have dim eyesight, a loss of hearing, and a weak voice. Fear will be exaggerated because the body won't be physically able to handle what it could in younger days.

All this is Solomon's morbid, yet accurate description of the aging process of the human body; and he even mentions the graying of hair when he says, "the almond tree will flourish." Solomon goes on with this dismal and discouraging discourse by saying it is a burden for the aged to pick up a grasshopper, meaning that work becomes a burdensome and almost impossible task. Even the desire for food will fail. At **this** point, there's virtually nothing left to bring excitement or pleasure to life. Solomon concludes by saying there is nothing in the future for someone in this condition except to go to the "long home," which is his way of describing death. Only the mourners remain to remind anyone of the dead. With an outlook like that, no wonder Solomon said, "Vanity, vanity, all is vanity."

Solomon then made some interesting observations of what happened in his day at death. Ecclesiastes 12:6 says, *"Or ever the silver cord be loosed, or the golden bowl be broken, or the pitcher be broken at the fountain, or the wheel broken at the cistern."*

At that time in the Middle East, a bridegroom didn't always give his bride a ring. Instead, he would give her a silver cord which she wore about her neck. When the husband died, the wife removed the silver cord and placed it on his body; and the silver cord was buried with him. When an individual died, the eldest son held over the head of the deceased a pottery bowl painted in some way with gold. This bowl was filled with fire and was broken by the son to indicate that the "broken" body, which would return to the dust, had released the spirit to ascend into the presence of God.

If the mourners touched either the body or the bier upon which the body was placed, they washed themselves with water. According to Jewish law, an individual was "unclean" if they touched a dead body or anything that body touched, so this washing was necessary. Afterward they broke the special pitcher containing the cleansing water and all the personal effects of the dead were burned. We understand now that God gave these laws to avoid the spreading of disease. The "wheel broken at the cistern" refers to the bier or wagon that carried the body. Certain designated men would "put their shoulder to the wheel" and move the body to the burial place.

In those days it was customary for everyone in town to attend a funeral. When a father died, these people became witnesses to a very important procedure. The birthright privileges were ceremonially passed on to whichever son had been designated to receive the double portion. Under normal circumstances this was the eldest son, who was now to be the "king" (leader) and "priest" (spiritual head) of the family in the stead of his father.

This son was customarily given a brightly colored robe, such as Jacob gave Joseph; and a key was placed on his shoulders. Then the "birthright" son would put his hands on the corpse and close the eyes of his father. All these things indicated the son's inheritance and new authority in the family. When God told Jacob to go to his son Joseph in Egypt, He said, "Joseph will put his hands on your eyes." Although Joseph was not the eldest son, the Lord confirmed with those words that Joseph was to receive the birthright and the double inheritance.

The prophet Isaiah refers to this ceremony when he speaks prophetically of Jesus, God's birthright Son:

> *And I will clothe him with thy robe, and strengthen him with thy girdle, and I will commit thy government into his hand: and he shall be a father to the inhabitants of Jerusalem, and to the house of Judah. And the key of the house of David will I lay upon his shoulder; so he shall open, and none shall shut; and he shall*

shut, and none shall open (Isaiah 22:21,22).

Now that I've told you everything you didn't want to hear about death and dying, let me tell you some wonderful news. Because Jesus died—and rose again—He had the right to pass the birthright privileges to every born-again believer. The same authority and power of Christ has been given to us as kings and priests in God's kingdom. (See Revelation 1:6.) Every believer has been clothed with a robe of righteousness; and Jesus Himself said, *"I will give unto thee the keys of the kingdom of heaven: and whatsoever thou shalt bind* [lock or close] *on earth shall be bound in heaven: and whatsoever thou shalt loose* [unlock or open] *on earth shall be loosed in heaven"* (see Matthew 16:19, Revelation 3:7):

> *For if by one man's offense death reigned by one;*
> *much more they which receive abundance of grace*
> *and of the gift of righteousness shall reign in life*
> *by one, Jesus Christ* (Romans 5:17).

Oh, what good news! We don't have to live and die *under the sun* we can live *under the Son* and die in victory. In Luke 10:19 Jesus said, *"Behold, I give unto you power to tread on serpents and scorpions, and over all the power of the enemy: and nothing shall by any means hurt you."* Life doesn't have to be a drag that just descends to the grave; in Christ, life can be a continual celebration which ascends into the very presence of God. You won't always be happy—you will encounter grief and pain—but you can always have the joy of the Lord which is your strength! (See Nehemiah 8:10.)

Did you know something supernatural happened to you when you were born again that absolutely changed and transformed your life? The Holy Ghost, that Spirit of life, is indwelling you. He witnesses to you that you are God's child, and He is continually quickening your *mortal* body.

The word *quicken* means "to make alive." If you have God's Spirit in you, with what kind of life are you being quickened? Your physical body is being made alive with God's life. No longer do you have to be ruled and dominated by the decaying process of your natural body; your body must submit to the supernatural life of God.

There is now, *right now*, a life-giving principle working in you which will sustain your body until the end. As you grow old, you don't have to have feeble knees, failing eyesight, loss of hearing, or a quavering voice. You don't have to be frightened at the slightest sound or exhausted with the smallest task. Life doesn't have to be that way for you under the SON because you have the Holy Spirit quickening your mortal body! Someday you will receive an immortal body, one that cannot die; but right now the Spirit of life can supernaturally sustain the mortal body that is going to die:

. . . *and as thy days, so shall thy strength be*
(Deuteronomy 33:25).

This is a concept almost too hard for our minds to grasp, but let me tell you of my own personal experience. I have more energy and more strength at 60 than I had in my twenties. When I was in my twenties, I was always whining and complaining about being tired.

My husband would come home and ask, "How are you?"

My stock answer was, "I'm so tired!" Because Wally got "so tired" of hearing those words, he said my theme song was, "I'm tired." He would really irritate me by singing to me an old song titled "Tired, I'm So Tired." I wanted to slap him.

To be sure, teaching school and being a homemaker kept me busy. But that schedule didn't begin to compare with my schedule today, and now I'm full of vigor and vitality!

What is the difference? In those days I was living life *under the sun*. I did not know how to live life *under the Son*; I didn't even know that kind of life was available. When I heard about the quality of life I could have in Christ, I began to appropriate that life; and I retired "tired." Today I'm not going "downhill"; I'm going "uphill"; and I intend to continue this upward climb until the day my body dies or Jesus takes me in the Rapture. You know, Christians shouldn't just be looking for healing; we should be expecting divine health. Every Christian should stay healthy!

HOW TO HAVE GIANT MENTALITY

In the 13th chapter of Numbers, a story of faith and a story of doubt are recorded. Moses sent twelve men to "spy" out the land which God had promised the Israelites. This preview of Canaan was intended to encourage the people with a report of all the good things God was giving to them. However, ten of these spies came back with an "evil" fear-filled report of Canaanite giants, who would surely keep Israel from the "Promised Land." Ten leaders of Israel saw themselves as grasshoppers before these "gigantic" problems. Because Joshua and Caleb believed the Word of God, they saw themselves as giants and the giants as grasshoppers. Only two men had a view of faith.

Joshua and Caleb stood before the people and said:

> . . . *The land, which we passed through to search it, is an exceeding good land. If the LORD delight in us, then he will bring us into this land, and give it us; a land which floweth with milk and honey. **Only rebel not** ye against the LORD, neither fear ye the people of the land; for they are bread for us: their defence is departed from them,*

and the LORD *is with us:* ***fear them not***
(Numbers 14:7-9).

Joshua and Caleb were fearlessly able to view themselves as the giants who could devour the people of Canaan. To them, these people were going to be "the breakfast food of champions." Joshua and Caleb were living life under the S-o-n! These two faith-filled men knew "it could be done"; Israel could take the land flowing with milk and honey. Instead of seeing giants, Caleb and Joshua saw the good land. They even brought back some of its bounty for the others to see. However, the towering obstacles obscured the good things from the view of most of Israel and caused the majority of the people to decide "it couldn't be done." You see, they were living life under the s-u-n.

Joshua and Caleb had *giant* mentality. Because they believed they could do anything God said they could do, they lived their lives in the supernatural! Joshua and Caleb looked at what God could do instead of what they couldn't do. These two men lived under the Son. The unbelieving crowd had "grasshopper" mentality; because they were overcome by every problem, they continued to live life in the natural. These people were so busy looking at what they couldn't do, they could never see what God could do. They lived under the sun.

Have you ever wondered why some Christians are more successful in life than others? It all depends on one's outlook—whether a person looks at life under the ***sun*** or whether a person looks at life under the ***Son***. Some people have "grasshopper" vision. They are so busy looking at what they aren't, they don't see what they can be in God. Those with "giant" vision see themselves as God sees them, and they become what they want to be. The first group is unsuccessful; the second group is successful. Even though you are a Christian, success only comes when you see yourself in the proper perspective and act accordingly. That's living under the Son.

This testimony from a woman, who wrote the ministry, is an example of someone with "giant" vision. The lady had been suffering with cancer and had severe pain in her back and in her lungs. Every day she listened to my TV program and said with me, "This is the best day of my life because Jesus lives big in me!" This woman had a "vision" of herself being healed and well. One day when I prayed for the sick, this woman s-t-r-e-t-c-h-e-d out her faith into the land of promise. Within two hours most of her pain was gone, and she was able to breath freely. She wrote, "Eleven months ago I wasn't supposed to live overnight, but God spared me and *I am being healed.*" This precious lady sees herself well. She is living life under the Son, and she will conquer this illness.

Let's go back to the "wilderness." God severely judged Israel's unbelief and told them they would wander in that wilderness 40 years until all the "grasshoppers" died. The unbelievers said they couldn't go into the land—and they didn't go into the land. God judged them by the words of their own mouths. There were Joshua and Caleb stuck with a bunch of whining cowards for 40 years. What were they going to do? They did exactly what Moses did; they stuck it out. Because they had a vision of promise, they were able to survive the wilderness experience. Caleb had walked all over the area of Hebron and claimed it as his own. He always looked forward to the day when Hebron would be his possession. Caleb told Moses that Hebron was the spot he wanted.

Caleb could have said, "What's the use, I'll never get Hebron. I'll wander around in this wilderness for 40 years, and then I'll die here. I'm 40 years old now; and by the time we spend 40 more years out here and another 5 or 6 years taking the land, I'll be at least 85 years old—too old to enjoy anything." However, Caleb didn't think that way. Even though he would be over 80 when Israel possessed Canaan, Caleb made a decision to live under the *Son* instead of under the *sun.* He decided that whatever time he would live in Hebron, it would still be wonderful. Caleb settled in for the "long haul" and determined that whatever came his way he would come through. You see, Caleb and Joshua had God's promise that they would enter the land; and they held tightly to that promise.

When a person is in church or when everything is going good, it's easy to say, "Glory to God, I'm going to live in the supernatural." Then when tomorrow comes and the bill collector is at the door, bad news arrives, you lose your job, your kids bring home bad grades, and your mate gets angry with you, what do you do? Are you going to live in the natural, observe all the "signs of the times," and be devoured by the giants? Or are you going to live in the supernatural, feast on God's Word, and devour your giants? Are you going to live life under the *sun* or live life under the *Son?*

Now let's see what Caleb had to come through. This man had to conquer "giants" in the wilderness before he ever faced the giants in Canaan. How would you like to be with 2 million, murmuring people for 40 years? Are you cool, calm, and collected when your boss gets angry with you or when your kids are fussing and complaining? We all have some idea of what Caleb faced; and yet, he set his face toward Canaan. Yes, Caleb had Moses, Aaron, and Joshua who were living in the supernatural. There was a faithful minority, which also included the younger generation; but this group was greatly outnumbered at first by the majority who were walking a purely natural path.

What about the climate? I don't think it would be too wonderful to spend 40 years in a desert. In order for the people to survive the climate, God provided a cloud by day, to shield them from the awful heat, and a pillar of fire by night, to warm them when the desert became extremely cold. There were also those poisonous snakes which caused the death of many Israelites. That's not to mention the other "critters" that were probably there. God always made a provision for the people, but the wilderness certainly was not paradise. And Caleb had to stay there with those unbelievers when they could all have been in Canaan.

Then there was that monotonous diet. We all enjoy variety in our diet, and these people were *no* exception. Food is a very important part of life. Not only is it nutritious but it is also enjoyable. Look at most of us, and you can see how much we enjoy food. Nevertheless, everyone can "burn out" on a particular food, and the Israelites had manna for breakfast, manna for lunch, and manna for dinner. If they wanted a snack between meals, it was manna. The manna could be baked, boiled, fried, and roasted; it could be mashed, toasted, and sliced—but it was still manna. I don't suppose there was much danger of the Israelites being overweight.

Maybe a few meals of manna would be fine, but 40 years of manna? Of course, the people complained about this; and the Lord supplied some quail. But many of them died when they ate the quail. It wasn't because the food was tainted; it was because their hearts were tainted. Finding an adequate supply of water was also a problem. The wilderness travelers often faced the lack of water; but God always came through, even with some miraculous demonstrations in spite of their complaints. So Caleb had a monotonous diet for 40 years, and he didn't always know where he would get his next drink of water; but he never let it affect his attitude of faith.

Caleb never let the detour of a wilderness experience detour him from living in the supernatural. This giant of faith always kept his attitude right with God. Although he wasn't living in the "lap of luxury" and there was murmuring and rebellion all around, Caleb was never moved from his position of life under the Son. Caleb was diligent about keeping his heart in the right place. Even though he had to wait and wait and wait for the promise, Caleb's spirit did not fail. Caleb's heart was established in God, and he was in for the "long haul" no matter how long that took. Because Caleb's spirit never failed, his strength never failed.

Remember, God's Word tells us to guard our hearts with all diligence because the issues of life come out of the heart. When Jesus said He had good news for the poor, He told the people that He was anointed to heal the broken hearted. You see, healing begins in the heart. Jesus didn't first talk to the people about healing their bodies; He talked about healing their hearts. If the attitude of the heart is right, the body can be healthy. But if the heart attitude is wrong, the body is subject to sickness. Even if you receive a miraculous healing, you can lose it if your attitude is wrong. It all begins with a heart that is right toward God. The way to live life under the Son is to have a right attitude. With wrong attitudes, you will only live life under the sun.

WHOLLY SERVE THE LORD!

What was the key to Caleb's life that brought him through? What kept his attitude right? I found three basic things that were vitally important to his success. First Caleb had seen the miraculous demonstration of the power of God. As a young man Caleb had seen the ten plagues that spoiled Egypt and spared Israel. He had seen the Red Sea open for God's people and close over their enemies, and he had seen an entire nation healed when they ate the lamb. In the wilderness, Caleb's experience with the miraculous included drinking the "sweet" water of Marah, water which gushed out from a rock, and eating manna from heaven. This man had encountered the supernatural—he knew that life was more than natural.

Secondly, Caleb believed the Word. While most of the Israelites were a people of natural provision, Caleb was a man of supernatural promise. God's Word didn't just go into Caleb's physical ears; it went into his heart. He believed, according to Deuteronomy 33:25, that God would supply the necessary physical strength for every day he lived. At Marah when the tree made the bitter water sweet, Caleb took to heart the revelation of Jehovah-rophe, "God your health." God's promise to bring His people into a land flowing with milk and honey anchored the hope in Caleb's heart. I can just hear Caleb say, "I'm not going down the drain because my health isn't going to fail and neither is my strength." Caleb made a decision to stand firmly on God's promises and live in the supernatural, no matter what any of the doubters said.

Every time you have to make a decision, are you going to listen to people or promises? Of course, you are going to listen to God's promises. They are going to enter through your eyes and ears and drop into your heart. Then you will walk in the supernatural and not be limited by the natural. Make one enormously important decision, and it will be your guide in making every other decision you will make. Just like Caleb, decide to live according to the Word of God and His promises. Say, "I'm going to believe the promises no matter what." People around you may not understand. They may not claim the promises; they may even try to explain them away. But those people will be living life under the sun while you enjoy life under the Son.

When we don't see God's answers right away, there is always a temptation to wonder how long we have to wait. For Caleb, it was 45 years. Are you willing to wait 45 years? Are you in for the "long haul"? Some people can't wait 45 seconds, 45 minutes, or even 45 hours. Don't ask them to wait 45 days and certainly not 45 months. Forty-five years? Forget it! One seasoned evangelist says if you are willing to wait forever, it won't take very long! In other words, the longer you have any questions about the ability of God's Word to bring your answer, the longer it will take. Caleb was convinced from the beginning, so he could wait 45 years. God's Word doesn't wear out with the passing of time; it is always potent and full of supernatural power.

I find that God's Word just gets better and better. That's because God's unchanging Word is changing me and making me better! If you are absolutely convinced that God's Word works, you won't be moved by time or circumstance. Instead, the Word will move you into better circumstances in every area of your life. The Word took Caleb into Canaan, didn't it? There he finally received Hebron as his inheritance. He didn't waste time moaning and groaning about the lost years. At 85 Caleb was able to conquer the giants and enjoy the remaining years of his life in the land which God had promised to him.

The third key to Caleb's ability to live life under the Son, is found in the mouths of four persons including Caleb himself. God testified that He would give Caleb and his children the land upon which Caleb had walked *because he* **wholly** *followed the Lord.* (See Deuteronomy 1:36.) Caleb's own words also testify of his faithfulness:

> *Forty years old was I when Moses the servant of the LORD sent me from Kadesh-barnea to espy out the land; and I brought him word again as it was in mine heart. Nevertheless my brethren that went up with me made the heart of the people melt: but I* **wholly** *followed the LORD my God* (Joshua 14:7,8).

Moses swore before all the people that the land where Caleb had walked would be his because Caleb had **wholly** followed the Lord (see Joshua 14:9); and Joshua wrote:

> *Hebron therefore became the inheritance of Caleb the son of Jephunneh the Kenezite unto this day, because that he* **wholly** *followed the LORD God of Israel* (Joshua 14:14).

Four times we find the phrase, "he wholly followed the Lord." The word *wholly* comes from the word *whole*, and means "complete," "entire," "full," or "total"; it is "without diminution." Caleb's heart was so full of the Word of God that the promises could never be diminished by doubt.

Caleb made a decision in his heart that he would wholly serve the Lord with his entire being: his spirit, his mind, his emotions, his will, and his body. Some people only want to serve God with their minds. Give them an intellectual sermon or an intellectual book, and they're fine; but if

God doesn't speak to their intellect, forget it! If the mental "appetite" isn't being satisfied, they aren't satisfied. They *know* a lot about God, but that's it.

Others only "feel" God. These people are moved to serve the Lord only by emotional experience. If they don't have "goose bumps" or "shivers" up their spines, it just can't be God. They can dance and shout at church; but when the "high" is over, you can't find them. When people who run on emotion "feel" good or they've had an answer to prayer or they've heard a great praise report, they "really love God." But when these people are at an emotional low, they may have a nervous breakdown.

Then there are those people who will do anything physical for God. Their bodies are the only part of them in the service of the Lord. They think they aren't serving God unless they are involved in some physical activity. This kind of person will set up tables, move chairs, sweep floors, and climb ladders for God. All that is wonderful; but don't ask these people to come to a prayer meeting, read their Bibles every day, or study the Word.

Love for God should be the motivation for serving Him. God has told us to love and serve Him with all our hearts, with all our souls, with all our minds, and with all our strength. That involves the whole person. God wants us wholly to serve Him. He knows if we serve Him only with our minds, we will become warped. He knows if we serve Him only with our emotions, we will get out of balance. And He knows if we serve Him only with our bodies, all we will get are muscles unless our hearts are right. Don't ever think the path to heaven is paved with our "good" works.

God loves us so much that He wants us to be whole people. When we are whole people, we will be holy people.

Without a holy walk, no person will see the Lord! (See Hebrews 12:14.) That means you must serve God with your mind. You may understand many things; but I guarantee that there will be things in life you won't understand. Are you going to throw away your faith when those things come along, or will you continue to be faithful? Some years ago our entire church put every ounce of faith we had into believing for a lovely 16-year-old who had leukemia—and she died. Because of a circumstance they didn't understand, a few people decided it wasn't always God's will to heal. However, one person heard this word from the Lord, "Don't have questions about Me in this matter; *you can't afford to doubt.* My child is now with me, but you are still on earth where faith is the only way to live!"

What about your emotions? When you *feel* like God is a million miles away and life is a "downer," are you going to give up? No, your emotions belong to God when you are wholly committed to Him. If you feel "up," that's great; but if you feel "down," it doesn't make any difference. God will come through for you because you are coming through for Him. Everyone of us experiences disappointments, but don't give the enemy any opportunity in your life just because your emotions are on a roller coaster. Command your emotions to get in line with God's Word and remain steady!

A young woman, who used to work in our ministry, married a man who seemed to be a totally committed Christian. However, as soon as they were married, things began to go "sour" and he became "another" person—angry, verbally abusive, and delinquent. Instead of falling apart, she took a stand of faith. When the situation seemed utterly hopeless and her emotions screamed for attention, she stood on God's promises. Eventually the couple separated, and he took employment in another city. But she didn't let go when she had every "earthly" reason to "hang it up." Nearly two years went by, but she never gave up. Then the husband came back to talk his wife into a divorce; but before he left, he had recommitted his life to the Lord and the marriage was restored. He said, "I never thought she would stick it out; but she is a woman of faith, not a woman of feelings." Praise the Lord! This husband is now wholly serving God, and he has been healed of the emotional abuse he suffered as a child.

Are we going to be "fair weather" Christians and serve our bodies instead of the Lord? Some people are into "works," but others are into comfort. Of course, they are in church—unless they are tired or the weather is bad. If you aren't feeling well, where do you belong? No, you don't belong in bed; you belong in church where you can receive prayer for healing! I know of a situation that really touched my heart. A young Christian woman, so full of life and vitality, was hit by a drunken driver; and she came out of the accident a paraplegic. Her mate didn't leave her as some do; instead he remained wholly dedicated to her and to the Lord. He works, does the housework and the cooking; he feeds her, bathes and dresses her—and the two of them attend every service at their church. Yes, they are believing for her healing; but in the meantime, they are wholly serving the Lord!

When I look at Caleb, I see that he kept his attitude right. He never had a nervous breakdown, and he never wore out physically. With his mind, his emotions, and his body, Caleb wholly served the Lord. Let's look at the outcome of this holy man. In Jeremiah 29:11 God says His thoughts toward us are good and not evil so He may give us a good future.

Although Jeremiah had not yet penned those words, Caleb knew the truth of them; and he wholly trusted the Lord with his future. When Israel entered Canaan, Caleb asked for the land of Hebron where he had walked 45 years before. This man knew God's promise to give him the land upon which he walked.

Joshua reminded Caleb that this mountainous country was the home of the giants. Undaunted, Caleb answered that he was as strong at 85 as he had been at 40; and if the Lord would be with him, he would drive out every giant. (See Joshua 14:11.) Joshua granted Caleb's request, and Caleb went up and took Hebron. Caleb didn't go part of the way; he went all the way. This man knew how to live life under the Son because he was wholly committed to God. He lived life in the supernatural and not in the natural. That's the way God expects everyone of us to live! We can all experience life *under the Son* instead of life *under the sun* when we wholly belong to the Lord.

Let's look at the ways in which Caleb wholly served the Lord. Caleb wholly believed; like Abraham he did not stagger at God's promise (see Romans 4:20). You, too, must fully believe as you wholly follow Him. If your mind belongs to the Lord, you can renew your mind with the Word of God and have the mind of Christ (see Romans 12:2; I Corinthians 2:16). You don't have to become senile; your mind can remain strong and healthy. Every change in your life can be a change for the better when your emotions are wholly God's. When you wholly commit your body to the Lord, you don't have to conform to the world; you will be conformed to God. Quit accepting the natural and step into the supernatural!

Caleb wholly witnessed with his life. Everything Caleb did

and said was a witness of his wholeness. His life was constant and unswerving. When the crowd would have stoned him for insisting they could take Canaan, he didn't say, "Put down that rock; maybe I'm wrong." There was no compromise in Caleb's life. He didn't care if it was a crowd of unbelievers or a crowd of giants, he didn't swerve from God's Word. Our lives also should wholly witness Christ. People should know that we are Christians. They should see a difference in our lifestyle. We should radiate such love that others want what we have. Are we as eager to share Jesus now as when we first met Him, or have we become sophisticated cowards who hide behind a myriad of excuses? Every person we meet is either on the way to heaven or on the way to hell! Jesus gave His life for them; have we wholly given our lives to Him?

Then Caleb wholly waited. For 45 years he kept his eyes on Hebron. He had supernatural eyesight. In the natural he could see snakes, desert, whining people, and manna; but he kept his eyes on what he *knew* was ahead. If we are to come into God's expected future for us, we must also keep our eyes on God's Word. Giants challenged Caleb, but they didn't prevent him from taking Hebron. Jewish history says that when the giants saw this 85-year-old man, they **retired**. Later Caleb *gave* Hebron as an offering to the Lord for a "city of refuge," although he kept the surrounding land. There is no doubt that we live in challenging times, but we can "retire" every "giant" the devil brings our way whether we are 25 or 85—when we wholly wait on God. I like it when our faith scares the devil! Is your life an offering to the Lord?

Did you know that Hebron means "fellowship?" Isn't it interesting that Caleb obtained Hebron after years of continual fellowship with God. That same kind of fellowship with God can be yours when you wholly follow the Lord. That means day by day you must be consistent with God in every area of your life. Each day you look to Him and say, "I'm wholly yours Lord: my spirit, my soul, my body is yours." If one day brings a defeat or disappointment, use it as an opportunity to gain another victory which will glorify the Lord. Daily remember that God will take every situation you give to Him and turn it to your good. After a while, this way of living becomes a habit. It's not a struggle, but it is spontaneous! Then you will realize you are every bit whole in Him—spirit, soul, and body. You are no longer living life *under the sun.* Now you are living life *under the Son!* It's God's victorious lifestyle for those wholly committed to Him.

Chapter Seven
ROOT IT UP!

The doctor stood at the woman's bedside shaking his head in unbelief. The facts were incredible; nevertheless, every test revealed no cancer in this woman's body. Two weeks ago the patient had been given only another 24 hours to live. Her husband had completed funeral arrangements, and the family had been notified. However, everything had changed since then. The happy doctor was looking now into the bright smiling face of a woman who was very much alive. Although there was no medical explanation for what had happened, the cancer was gone; and she was being discharged! The medical chart read, "Cancer in remission."

Everyone involved in this situation was baffled by the woman's mysterious healing—except one individual who believed in God's marvelous power to heal. This person had never met the "dying" woman, but she had heard of the woman's plight through a friend. Fierce anger and intense hope had risen up inside her like a geyser—anger at the devil's disease and hope in God's ability to heal. There was no question in her mind as to either Satan's intention or God's intention. Jesus defined both purposes in John 10:10 when He said: *"The thief cometh not, but for to steal, and to kill, and to destroy: I am come that they might have life, and that they might have it more abundantly."*

The woman prayed, "You foul spirit of cancer, leave this woman's body. I curse you in Jesus' name, and I command this cancer to die at the roots. It shall find no place in this body to stay." Within the critical 24 hours, the "dying" woman reported to her friend that she could feel something moving about in her body. Even the friend could feel the movement when she placed her hands on the woman's abdomen. This was strange indeed, but the woman was feeling better. In a day or two the patient, who was still alive, began to vomit large quantities of some odd substance. When the vomiting ceased, the woman began a remarkable recovery. All the doctors could say when the lab tests came back clear was, "She vomited the cancer from her body."

This amazing recovery came to my attention because the lady who prayed was a friend of mine. I know the facts surrounding this case seem unbelievable, but so does the record of Jesus' encounter with a fig tree in Mark 11:12-21. Let me refresh your memory. One day Jesus was hungry so He decided to eat fruit from the fig tree. When He found no figs, He spoke to the tree saying, *". . . No man eat fruit of thee hereafter for ever. . . ."* The next day Jesus' disciples were astonished to see that the fig tree was dead, *dried up from the roots.* Peter said, *". . . Master, behold, the fig tree which thou **cursedst** is withered away."*

You may say, "Well, that was Jesus; He can do anything." Listen to Jesus' response to His disciples:

> *. . . Have faith in God. For verily I say **unto you**, That whosoever shall **say** unto this mountain, Be thou removed, and be thou cast into the sea; and **shall not doubt** in his heart, but shall **believe** that those things which he **saith** shall come to pass; he shall have whatsoever he **saith*** (Mark 11:22,23).

Jesus has given power to believers, if they do not doubt but believe what they say, to curse roots and move mountains. Are you a believer or are you a doubter?

Jesus and His disciples were near the Mount of Olives when He spoke that promise, but we know He doesn't expect us to go around cursing tree roots or moving mountains—unless they are in the way of God's purpose. He does expect us to root up problems (such as cancer) and move the mountains of difficulty in our lives. In Matthew 15:13 Jesus said, " . . . *Every plant, which my heavenly Father hath not planted, shall be* **rooted up**." We can begin by rooting up personal fears and doubts. We do this by planting the faith-producing Word in our hearts. Then in the authority of Jesus' name, we can root up sickness, disease, infirmity, and all manner of evil which our Lord certainly has not planted.

Incidentally, in case you have any question about "mountain-moving" faith, I must tell you this true story. A missionary in India taught at a girls' school which was located under the shadow of a mountain. The sun never reached the girls' dormitory; consequently, it was cold and dank and their laundry wouldn't dry properly. One day the missionary taught the passage in Mark 11. Right then the students decided to believe "their" mountain would be removed. The girls prayed with great expectancy, although their teacher didn't encourage them because she didn't want their faith crushed. In just a few days, the astonished missionary saw giant earth movers taking huge "bites" from the mountain which was in the way of a government project. The mountain was removed, but Jesus' little disciples were not surprised.

In the Scriptures we read that God's commission overwhelmed the prophet Jeremiah. At the time, the young man considered himself to be only a child who could not speak for the Lord with any measure of authority. However, the Lord told Jeremiah:

> . . . *Say not, I am a child: for thou shalt go to all that I shall send thee, and whatsoever I command*

149

> *thee thou shalt speak. Then the LORD put forth his*
> *hand, and touched my mouth. And the LORD said*
> *unto me, Behold, I have put* **my words** *in thy*
> *mouth. See, I have this day set thee over the*
> *nations and over the kingdoms, to* **root out***, and*
> *to pull down, and to destroy, and to throw down,*
> **to build, and to plant** (Jeremiah 1:7,9,10).

We know that Jeremiah became a mighty "mouthpiece" for God. God used him to root out and expose much evil in Israel, and Jeremiah turned many to righteousness.

One of the most interesting testimonies that has come into our ministry was from a man who lives in South Dakota. He farms the same land his father and grandfather and great-grandfather farmed before him. So the land has belonged to this family for four generations, but before that it belonged to the Indians from whom it had been purchased. Every year the farmer battled a poisonous weed which would kill the cattle if they ate very much of it. At best, the weed made the cattle quite ill. This little weed was costing the man a great deal of money because the land had to be sprayed by a crop duster every season.

Despite all this effort the root system of the poisonous plant was never killed. Then when studying the history of this area, the farmer discovered that long ago the Indians had put a curse on the land. Being Christians, the farmer and his wife began to fast and pray to break this curse. The two of them would drive around their property and command the root system of the weeds to die. There was no change for a season or two, but the farmer and his wife stood firm and didn't give up. The couple kept trusting God and confessing that the poisonous weeds were dead at the roots.

One spring morning the farmer's young son went out and

pulled up one of the weeds which were already growing again. The plant looked as though it was thriving—*but the roots were shriveled and dry.* Every weed they examined was the same way; they had all died at the roots. Although the neighboring farmers continued to battle the obnoxious weed, this man never had the weeds on his property again. You see, Jesus said that everything that wasn't planted by God would be rooted up. Most assuredly, the poisonous weed was not planted by God. This man believed the promise and acted accordingly. Now he is rid of the costly nuisance.

Let me tell you that if you have cancer, it didn't come from God. If you are sick or disabled with any kind of condition, God did not plant that thing in your life. If God didn't plant these destructive things, then who did and what are you supposed to do about them? Satan is the one who sows the weeds, and the weeds need to be pulled. (See Matthew 13:28,30.) Root it up! Get ahold of that thing with the Word of God on your tongue. Curse it at the roots, and it has to die. Just like the weeds on the farmer's land, it may not happen instantly, but it will happen. The tree Jesus cursed at the roots showed no immediate signs of death, but a day later the tree was dead.

IS FAITH NECESSARY FOR HEALING?

I want to answer some questions that are often asked on the subject of healing. If I root out doubts you may have concerning healing, then I can plant good seeds of faith in your heart. My goal is to enable you to believe that anything is possible with God.

Faith is the issue of the first question. Is some faith always needed in order for a person to be healed? Although this matter has been discussed previously in the book, such a question is worth our attention here. We've looked at some circumstances when it wasn't apparent that faith was present in the individual who was healed, but we can't say there wasn't someone exercising faith. For example, no one knew somebody was exercising faith for the woman dying of cancer. Her cure was unexplainable to all those concerned. Nevertheless, mighty faith was in operation:

But let him ask in faith, nothing wavering. For he that wavereth is like a wave of the sea driven with the wind and tossed. For let not that man think that he shall receive any thing of the Lord. A double minded man is unstable in all his ways (James 1:6-8).

James tells us here that any individual who wavers between faith and doubt can never really believe in order to receive. Remember that Jesus Himself could do no mighty works in his hometown because of the people's unbelief. That unbelief became a strong wall that even Jesus' power could not penetrate. It wasn't that power wasn't present, but faith was not present in most of those in Nazareth. Only a few sickly folk were healed. The original text indicates that only minor ailments were cured.

Paul perceived that a crippled man in Lystra had *faith* to be healed. (See Acts 14:8-10.) I'm certain there were numerous cripples in Lystra; and if Paul's compassion could have healed them, they all would have gotten up and walked. However, only one man was made whole when he mixed faith with the Word which Paul preached. Then there was an agreement of faith. When Paul commanded the cripple to stand, the man's feet and legs received strength and he leaped and walked. This connection of faith produced great results because the power to heal is released when two or more agree *in faith*. (See Matthew 18:19.) Several people agreed in faith for their friend whom Jesus healed when they lowered him through a roof into Jesus' presence.

Still others believed when no one around could "see" what they saw with eyes of faith. There was the woman with an issue of blood, blind Bartimaeus, and a lame man at the Temple gate. Those who came for others included the father with a dying daughter and the centurion who came to Jesus for his servant. We could list others, but in every case Jesus said the healing resulted when someone had faith in His healing power. I like to think of God's power as a stick of dynamite and faith as the fire that lights it. Incidentally, the Greek word translated *power* in the New Testament is *dunamis* from which we get the word dyanamite.

I know there have been times when God has told me to use my faith for someone who didn't have faith. These persons were often so tired and weary that their faith was completely drained; but I would tell them to lean on my faith, and they were healed. When they were unable to ignite the dynamite, I had the match and together we released God's power. Whether it is one's own faith or faith by "proxy" that connects with the Lord's power to heal, it is still faith. When God's Word lets us know that we can't please Him without faith, then I must conclude that faith is of vital importance when it comes to healing.

For what reason would anyone who loves Jesus want to neglect faith? Well, the enemy comes in and plants seeds of doubt in people's minds to make them think they can never have the kind of faith necessary for healing. Those seeds sprout and grow roots that need to be pulled. Sometimes faith wears thin in a severe trial when the answer doesn't come immediately, and discouraged people turn loose of faith. However, faith can always be encouraged by others and renewed through the Word of God. The promises are a never-ending source of supply, so God's children don't have to run dry.

One evening a gentleman in our congregation was having severe pain in his feet, and he stood for healing prayer. After the service his feet hurt worse than they had before. Did the man say, "Well, I guess it isn't going to work for me?" No indeed! Although the man could scarcely stand due to the pain, he kept standing on the Word of God. For a week the man continued to tell his feet they were healed. In the next service he attended, I received a word of knowledge about someone's feet being healed; and it was for this man. He later testified that his feet were healed at that moment. The problem was rooted out and the pain was gone.

This reminds me of an evangelist who was doing a seminar on healing—but he could barely get to the platform because of severe pain from a plantar wart on his foot. How embarrassing! He prayed and prayed, but nothing happened. He complained to God about the matter . . . nothing. He reminded God that this should be embarrassing to Him too . . . still nothing. One day after a service, the man was in agony and the Lord spoke to him, "Ask that young man over there to pray for your foot."

Now this young man was mentally retarded, so the evangelist argued with God. The Lord said, "Fine, it's your foot!" You can guess the outcome—the preacher surrendered, the young man prayed, and the foot was healed. In telling the story later, the man said, "The devil *planted* that plantar wart, but through humble faith God rooted it out."

DOES GOD HEAL CHILDREN OF UNSAVED PARENTS?

Do children of unsaved parents get healed? Does God heal sinners? Yes, the unsaved are often healed in meetings where the atmosphere is charged with faith. Of course, the sinner also may have exercised a measure of faith by attending the meeting. I've known unbelievers to be healed when people of faith prayed for them. It may have been for a mate, a child, a loved one, or a neighbor. Those who receive healing may go out and sin some more, but they can never forget that God healed them. That person has had an encounter with God and with His power that can't be denied. I believe the Lord will eventually get that sinner. The entire family of one of our pastors was born again when an unsaved grandmother was miraculously healed by God.

Although I believe that children of unsaved parents can be healed when someone of faith prays for them, I know that most of the time children are not healed when their parents are unbelievers. God has made parents responsible for their innocent offspring; and if there is no one to believe, how can healing take place? This is tragic, but true. Children don't know to have faith unless they have met Jesus through someone. I've even heard of children having visions of Jesus; but I believe that either someone was praying for them or they were reaching out to God. There is no question that children are very dear to God's heart.

King David lost his first son by Bath-sheba because of unrepented sin in his life. Jeroboam, who was first to rule the northern kingdom of Israel, lost a child because of sin in his life. This man set up a terrible system of idolatry in his nation in order to keep the men of Israel from attending the feasts at the Jerusalem Temple in the southern kingdom of Judah. The king feared losing the men's allegiance, so he pulled them away from their allegiance to God. Jeroboam turned from the Lord when he became nervous about losing a kingdom which God had given to him. This man didn't realize he was sacrificing his own son for a kingdom.

When King Jeroboam's son became critically ill, the king was frantic. Like most parents, he loved his son. The distraught king had his queen disguise herself and go to a prophet to ask if the child would live. The old blind prophet Ahijah, who had prophesied that Jeroboam would rule Israel, knew by the Spirit of God that it was the queen. The Lord had already given Ahijah a message for her. Ahijah said:

> *Arise thou therefore, get thee to thine own house: and when thy feet enter into the city, the child shall die. And all Israel shall mourn for him, and bury him: for he only of Jeroboam shall come to the grave,* **because in him there is found some good thing toward the LORD God of Israel in the house of Jeroboam** (I Kings 14:12,13).

That seems like a strange message, doesn't it? The child was going to die because God saw something good in him. Let's examine this situation. God loved this child in whom He saw goodness. Therefore, he didn't want Jeroboam's son to grow up in a household of sin and become an idolater. God did not intervene by healing the child, and so the child died. I don't want you to misunderstand me here. God *did not* put the illness on Jeroboam's son. In order to do that, God would have had to borrow sickness from the devil. Nevertheless, while this precious child was still innocent, God delivered him from the evil influence and took the child to Himself. This good boy was spared an eternity in hell.

Jeroboam's son died because of the sins of his mother and father. Parents who are ungodly bring tragedy, sickness, and death upon their own children. The Scriptures say that the sins of the fathers are visited on the children to at least the third and fourth generation (Numbers 14:18). This is a terrible truth, but what can children learn in ungodly homes but ungodliness? However, youngsters brought up in the nurture and admonition of the Lord learn godliness. Blessings follow their generations. If you are a parent, I'm going to tell you your faith can heal your children or your lack of faith can kill your children. Don't blame the death of a child on God. God is not a baby killer.

I believe that the Lord is particularly interested in the precious life of innocent children:

> *Take heed that ye despise not one of these little ones; for I say unto you, That in heaven their angels do always behold the face of my Father which is in heaven* (Matthew 18:10).

Three of the gospel writers recorded Jesus' awesome words of warning when He said that if anyone offends a child who believes in Him, it would be better for that person to have a millstone hung about his neck and then be thrown into the sea to drown.

If the Lord cares so much for children, then He is certainly ready to heal them. God delights to heal children when they are sick, but someone needs to have faith for them. The Lord has entrusted these little lives into the hands of parents who are responsible for training and molding them, as well as protecting them from both natural and spiritual evil. What normal parents would not want to provide for their children and keep them healthy when it is within their power to do so? God the Father is no different with His children, especially the little ones who are so vulnerable.

When the Syrophoenician woman—a gentile—came to Jesus and asked Him to heal her demonized daughter, Jesus told her that healing was the children's bread. The children to whom Jesus referred were the sons and daughters of Abraham. Nevertheless, this undaunted woman, who was considered a ''dog'' by the Jews, said that even little puppies can eat the crumbs which fall from the table. She was willing to pick up a few ''crumbs off the floor'' for her daughter. Although she wasn't a Jew, Jesus honored her persistent faith and the child was healed.

Parents, it is your job to provide healing bread for your children just as this mother provided healing bread for her daughter. We need to believe the Lord for our children's healing. Where there is no faith involved, there is sickness and premature death. Of course, we need to teach our children about healing. They need to learn the Scriptures that promise healing to them. Children so readily believe what they are taught—let's make sure we teach them righteousness. Where there is much sin involved, a child may die while they are still innocent and be removed from the awful contamination of sin.

ONCE A PERSON IS HEALED, CAN SICKNESS RETURN?

Can an affliction come back on a person who was *really* healed? Third John 2 gives us a clue:

*Beloved, I wish above all things that thou mayest prosper and be in health, **even as thy soul prospereth**.*

158

Health and healing are tied in with soul prosperity; if you are sick in your soul, you won't be well in body very long even if you've had a miraculous healing. Your mind must be established on the Word of God; your emotions must be controlled by the Lord; and your choices must be made according to God's principles. That is living in soul prosperity. Anything else brings sickness to the soul and sickness to the body.

The devil is always "lurking in the wings" to do anything he can to harm you. He will gladly put sickness back on your body if you give him the opportunity to do so. Affliction can come back when a person begins to walk with the devil instead of walking with the Lord. Anyone who gets out of faith is open for another attack of the enemy. Unless you continue to live in soul prosperity, the enemy can come back. Jesus overcame Satan's temptations with the Word of God, and that is the same way you need to resist him. Of course, Jesus was living a life of righteousness and so must you. Does that mean you must never sin to stay healed? No, but you must repent of known sin in your life. Go to the mirror of God's Word, and it will show you any sin.

John 5:14 tells of a man whom Jesus healed of an infirmity which had totally incapacitated the man for 38 years. The Lord's healing power was so mighty that it instantly drove out an affliction which had bound this man for nearly four decades. Nevertheless, Jesus told the man to go and sin no more before something even worse came upon him. Jesus was telling the man that sin would open the door to more sickness.

Do you recall that Jesus forgave the sins of the man lowered through a roof before He healed the man's body? Jesus knew that the man needed to live in soul prosperity so he could live in physical prosperity. Don't you know that man thought twice before he ever again indulged in sin!

In Luke 11:24-26 Jesus describes how evil spirits can enter a person who once was delivered:

> *When the unclean spirit is gone out of a man, he walketh through dry places, seeking rest; and finding none, he saith, I will return unto my house whence I came out. And when he cometh, **he findeth it swept and garnished**. Then goeth he, and taketh to him seven other spirits more wicked than himself; and they enter in, and dwell there: and the last state of that man is worse than the first.*

What is Jesus saying here? For one thing, He tells us that demons seek residence in people. These demons can have their bags packed with all sorts of disease and infirmity. Jesus healed an infirm woman who had been bent over for 18 years, and He said the woman should be "loosed from the bondage of Satan" (see Luke 13:16).

Specifically, Jesus told about the man with demons to illustrate that if we do not fill ourselves with the Word of God after we are free, something much worse can happen to us. Although the man in Jesus' illustration was clean, he was empty. By not filling the empty space with God, the man just hung a "vacancy" sign on himself. The demon and his companions were waiting for the opportunity to enter the man and gain a stronghold. Then the man was in worse condition than before. You cannot be a spiritual vacuum; either you will fill your soul with the spiritual things of God, or Satan will fill you with things from his spirit realm. Never forget that if the devil can find a place in you, he will take it!

When God says in Nahum 1:9 that " . . . *affliction shall*

not rise up the second time," we should understand two things: sickness may try to return, but it is never the Lord's will for this to happen. Jesus paid an awful price for our healing; and it should be obvious that God not only wants to heal His people, He wants them to stay healed and continue to live in health. When Jesus healed the boy who was having seizures, He said, " . . . *Thou dumb and deaf spirit, I charge thee, come out of him, and **enter no more into him**"* (Mark 9:25). You have the power in Jesus' name to tell sickness and disease that it cannot come back again! When I receive healing, I tell the devil that he will never put that sickness back on me and then I quote Nahum 1:9 to him. Satan probably knows the Word better than I do; but I remind him that I know it too, and I know that it works.

When young David knocked down Goliath, David finished the job by cutting off the giant's head. He was taking no chance that his enemy would get back up. I guarantee you that Goliath certainly wasn't going anyplace without his head—not on his own power anyway. When you knock down the devil, cut off his head! Tell him there is no way he is going to bring that affliction back to you, and he isn't bringing any other affliction either. It grieves me when people get healed of cancer and then six months or a year later they die. Doctors find absolutely no cancer cells in these patients; they are in total remission, and yet cancer attacks them again. We can stop this sort of thing, and we must stop it in Jesus' name.

I have people tell me they have a history of some condition or another, or they say some physical problem has been passed through their family for generations. I don't care about the past history; I'm concerned with the future. Stop that evil thing and pass it back to the devil. If he wants to play ball, show him you're on the winning team! God didn't plant sinus trouble in your life or cancer or heart disease or back problems. Root them out with the Word of God, and stand guard over your property:

> *And ye shall serve the LORD your God, and he shall bless thy bread, and thy water; and I will take sickness away from the midst of thee* (Exodus 23:24).

You see, there is a condition to soul prosperity and healing that lasts; *it is found in serving the Lord*.

CAN WE USE "POINTS OF CONTACT" TO HEAL?

What about things like anointing oil, prayer cloths, laying on of hands, touching a TV; do these have the power to heal? What is the purpose of such things?

When our ministry sends out letters containing a "prayer cloth," I've noticed that we get more response than at any other time. Testimony after testimony of miraculous healing come flooding back to us. We also get the most critical mail at this time because there are many folks who do not understand this sort of thing. They think it is just a very unspiritual gimmick.

But what about the testimony of the Scriptures? Naaman was healed of leprosy when he dipped in the Jordan seven times. God answered Gideon through a sheep skin, and Hezekiah with a sun dial. People were healed when the shadow of Peter fell on them; pieces of cloth taken from Paul's body healed others. Even the Lord Jesus used a "gimmick" when He put a spit ball on a blind man's eyes and then told him to go wash it off. You can't knock results; the man was healed! And what about the "laying on of hands" commanded by Jesus, and the anointing of oil spoken of by James? We need to find the practical truth here that will help our understanding of these unusual things which can be aids to healing.

God tells us in Psalms 103:14 that He knows our frame; He understands that our bodies are made of dust. May I add that the five physical senses are in the body. We are all very much see, hear, taste, smell, and touch people. Is it so unusual that the Lord would involve our senses in order to effect healing in our bodies? I think it is just like God to get the spirit, the soul, and the body working together in healing. If our senses are so unspiritual, then why did the Lord give them to us? It's the way we use our senses that can bring unspirituality and sin. No doubt our senses can tantalize us to sin, but they can also draw us to God. Doesn't Psalms 19:1 say, *"The heavens declare the glory of God; and the firmament sheweth his handywork"*? How are you going to know they are there if you can't see them?

I suppose one of the most criticized of all "aids" to healing is "put your hand on the TV." Can a television heal anyone, even if a person greatly used of God to heal the sick is speaking through the "tube"? If the TV could heal, then all we'd need to do is just set up TVs in church and tell people to touch them. Then what does happen when people receive healing in this manner? The TV is simply a point of contact for faith. Faith seems to rise in people when their senses are involved through some *point of contact,* but they are not healed by TVs, prayer cloths, oil, or hands. However, there is a holy anointing on any such item when it has been consecrated to the Lord for the purpose of healing.

Our church youth pastor was suffering so badly with a sinus infection that he stayed home from work one day.

While he was home, he took the opportunity to watch a man on TV who has a healing ministry. At one point this man said, "If you are suffering in your body right now, touch your TV and believe with me for your healing." The pastor thought, "What do I have to lose? I'm so miserable I'll do it." At the very moment he put his hands on the TV, the minister said, "There's someone watching who is suffering terribly with a severe sinus infection, and that person is being healed right now." Our youth pastor felt the power of God go through him, and instantly his sinus passages began to drain. He was at work the next day!

Probably the most effective point of contact in healing is the laying on of hands. I have seen more people healed when others laid hands on them than any other way. Many times I have laid hands on people who were sick, and I think I felt worse than they did. Nevertheless, they received their healing. It wasn't my healthy hands that healed them. However, my hands were a faith contact for those individuals. I had faith for their healing based on the Word of God, and they believed they would be healed when I put my hands on them. Sometimes when these persons were healed, I received my healing as well. Why? Because the prayer of faith, coupled with their healing, strengthened my faith to be healed. Folks, don't put God in a box; allow Him to flow according to His will.

CAN THE DEVIL HEAL PEOPLE?

Can the devil heal? Does he have the power to heal sick bodies? One time when Jesus cast a demon out of a person, some of the bystanders accused Him of doing it by the power of Satan. They said, *"He casteth out devils through Beelzebub the chief of the devils."* Jesus answered:

> . . . *Every kingdom divided against itself is*
> *brought to desolation; and a house divided against*
> *a house falleth. If Satan also be divided against*
> *himself, how shall his kingdom stand? because ye*
> *say that I cast out devils through Beelzebub. But*
> *if I with the finger of God cast out devils, no*
> *doubt the kingdom of God is come upon you*
> (Luke 11:17,18,20).

Jesus made it quite clear that Satan would be tearing apart his own kingdom if he were to do any good work such as healing or casting out devils. Satan's kingdom is full of sickness, death, and destruction; not health, life, and prosperity. Jesus said good things belong to God's kingdom.

Examine the book of Job and you will find that it was not God who brought all the calamity into Job's life, *it was the devil*. (See Job 1:12.) It is often debated whether God removed the protective hedge around Job or whether Job removed it himself through fear or self-righteousness. I just know the Lord allowed Satan the opportunity to attack Job. Nevertheless, God called Job an upright man who feared God and hated evil. In the trial Job never cursed God, and in the end God blessed Job with twice as much as he had before (see Job 42:10).

James 1:13-15 instructs us never to accuse God of being the author of the tests and trials in our lives, because His acts are never evil:

> *Every good gift and every perfect gift is from*
> *above, and cometh down from the Father of lights,*
> *with whom is no variableness, neither shadow of*
> *turning* (James 1:17).

Just as there is never any change in God, there is never any change in the devil. He is *always* the bearer of bad tidings such as sickness and disease, while God is *always* the bearer of good tidings such as healing and health! James does tell us that people are led into tests and trials when they succumb to their own lusts. Beware that you do not give Satan opportunity in your life.

If Jesus isn't healing by the power of God, it isn't being done. Jesus said He came to undo all the works of the devil:

> *How God anointed Jesus of Nazareth with the*
> *Holy Ghost and with power: who went about*
> *doing good, and healing all that were oppressed*
> *of the devil; for God was with him* (Acts 10:38).

The infallible Word says Jesus is the healer and the devil is the oppressor. Don't ever allow Satan to confuse you on this point. The people of Jonestown did, and over a thousand of them died when they followed "another savior."

We often hear or read about miraculous healings that have come from fountains or mountains, visions or apparitions. Let me say again that if the healing isn't being done by the power of the only true God in the name of His Son Jesus Christ of Nazareth, then there is something wrong at the root of the thing, no matter how good it may seem. When you're confused by these things, get to the root. If God hasn't planted it, it doesn't have good roots. If Jesus isn't glorified as God manifested in the flesh, then a counterfeit work is being performed by Satan. Always find where Jesus fits into the picture. Remember that Satan comes as an angel of light, and Paul said not to believe if even an angel came preaching "another" gospel. (See II Corinthians 11:14; Galatians 1:8.)

There is no question that some people get healed when they go to a shrine or some other place where healing is purported to be taking place. Nevertheless, I'm convinced that healing doesn't happen by going to a shrine, getting into certain pools, or traveling to where people have seen a "vision." However, people have been healed in certain instances; and I'm convinced it's because they put their faith in Jesus. Perhaps even without knowing it, they have looked beyond "their" point of contact to the only One Who heals.

It is also possible that some have had angelic visitations, and I know of verified instances when people have seen Jesus. Although there are scriptural accounts of angelic visitations when the persons who saw them were unaware of their true identity, I know of no instance when these heavenly messengers brought healing.

On the basis of scripture, I do know it is impossible for someone who has died to appear to the living, no matter how venerated that person may be. In Luke 16:19-31 Jesus told about a rich man in hell who pleaded with Abraham to send the beggar Lazarus from paradise to warn the rich man's ungodly brothers of their impending doom. However, the rich man was told that the living must accept God's Word to receive salvation. Jesus was restating the teaching of the Old Testament that we must seek God's direction, not the spirits of the dead. (See Deuteronomy 18:9-14 and Isaiah 8:19.)

I'm sure you've heard the accounts of untrained people in places like Mexico or South America who heal people by doing bloodless surgery with filthy knives. Witch doctors of Africa and some islands appear to heal with charms and potions. Satan has great spiritual power, and he may temporarily remove a sickness or torment which he has placed on a body; but he has no *creative* power to heal. He never has had this kind of power, and he never will! Those who are duped into thinking there is a difference between "white" magic and "black" magic are dreadfully mistaken.

It is all from the devil.

WHY DO SOME PEOPLE
DIE PREMATURELY?

What about the people who die short of their length of days? Do we have any answers? Well, in some instances I believe those who die as a result of illness get a glimpse of heaven; and they choose to go on over to the other side. I've heard testimonies of men and women who had death experiences and did not want to return; but because someone was praying fervently and effectively, the Lord sent them back. Some who die become so tired and weakened in the struggle to live that they find themselves unable to continue in the fight of faith.

Recently, a well-known pastor lost a battle with cancer, but a personal friend of his told me that the man wanted to go on home. Children may die because of unbelieving parents, others die because they are in the realm of fear and doubt, and some die because they are not walking in soul prosperity. Still others die, and none of us this side of eternity will ever know why; but we don't quit trusting God. Job had no idea that it was Satan who brought all his trouble, but he could still say of God, *"Though He slay me, yet will I trust him: . . . "* (Job 13:15).

We can't deny that people who receive prayer for healing are not always healed; they may even die. I don't have all the answers and neither does any other person, but I'm not going to stop praying and believing the Lord to touch people with His healing power. If I saw only a few people receive their healing or be raised from a death bed, I'd still keep praying for the sick. It is a scriptural thing to do, and I'm happy to report that we continually see more healed than are not healed! The more accurately the Body of Christ walks in the power of God, the more we see healing take place. Don't ever allow what looks like a failure to dampen your zeal to pray a healing prayer for yourself and others. Remember, according to James 5:15 the prayer of faith will save (deliver, redeem, and heal) the sick and the Lord will raise them up!

Chapter Eight
NAME THAT PROBLEM

It was "only" a dream, but it was a *spiritual* dream with a profound meaning. My friend knew the moment she awakened that the Lord had a message for her. In the dream this woman was teaching a group of people. During the time of instruction, she raised her arm and pointed to a "whatnot" shelf on the wall where there were a number of objects. When she did this, everything on the shelf began to shake and rattle; but in a few moments, they all became still. Again the woman raised her arm and pointed at one particular object on the shelf. This time the object to which she pointed lifted from the shelf, moved across the room suspended in midair, and came to rest in her outstretched hand. As the lady pondered the events in the dream, the Lord made quite clear what He wanted her to know, "Be specific when you pray, and you will get specific results."

I want to say that same thing to you now, "Be specific when you pray and you will get specific results!" Broad, general prayers, which I call "generic" prayers, may shake things a little; but they don't bring results. If you pray for nothing in particular, that's exactly what you'll get: nothing in particular! The more specifically you use your faith, the more specific will be the results. It is very important to identify the problem or situation on which you use your faith. Be specific in the *way* you pray, and be specific about *what* you pray. Both are very important.

Do you remember the old TV show called "Name That Tune"? On the program the player who guessed the title of the "mystery" tune received a prize. Only a fragment of an obscure song was played for the contestant, and so it was quite difficult to win the prize. Do you get the point? God isn't playing guessing games with us. We aren't naming tunes, but we do need to be accurate and definitive when naming the needs in our lives. When we pray specifically about them, we will receive the results we desire. Answered prayer is a good "prize" to be won. You know, some people pray, "Lord bless everybody." The Lord can't do much with a prayer like that.

What does it mean to be specific in the way you pray? The most important ingredient in any prayer should be the Word of God—or at least, the knowledge that what you pray is the will of God. I like to pray the Word back to the Father in Jesus' name. I know God will always honor the promises of His Word when it is prayed in faith. Of course, faith is the next ingredient. The Lord told a noted evangelist not to pray unless he knew when he prayed that the answer was forthcoming. This man said it drastically abbreviated his prayer life and changed nearly all of it. One time the Lord told me not to waste His time or mine by praying unbelieving, ineffective prayers.

Next, get right to the heart of a matter. The kind of prayer you pray is very important. In other words if someone is demon oppressed, a prayer for healing will not be too effective. You need to bind the demonic activity, and it is of great benefit to deal with the particular kind of oppression involved. When an individual's business is on the verge of bankruptcy, don't just ask the Lord to heal the business. Learn all you can about the specifics which brought the business to this point, and deal with every one of them when you pray about the matter. If you are praying about a broken relationship in your life, then examine your own heart, settle anything that needs to be settled there, and deal with the obvious things that brought about the problem.

Ask the Holy Spirit to show you things that may be pertinent to any prayer you pray. One of the most effective prayers I know in this regard was prayed by Paul in Ephesians 1:17. I make it personal every day. "Lord, give me the spirit of wisdom and revelation in the knowledge of Christ." Paul assures us in I Corinthians 1:30 that Christ Jesus is made unto us wisdom. We need the Lord's wisdom to know how to pray and what to pray. That wisdom is promised to us.

Paul was a giant in prayer, and the results in his life prove it. This man strongly recommended praying with the Holy Spirit. Do you want to pray the perfect will of God concerning each matter? In Romans 8:27 Paul says that the Holy Spirit intercedes for us according to the will of God. Verse 28 tells us that when we pray the will of God, He is able to work all the things in our life for good. Pray with the Spirit, and God will turn around that problem for you! In Ephesians 6:18 Paul wrote, *"Praying always with all prayer and supplication in the Spirit, ..."* I'm convinced that praying in tongues helps prioritize the needs and issues in your prayer time.

TORMENTS, PLAGUES, AND OPPRESSIONS

Now, I want to look at six basic things that Jesus identifies as sickness. In order to obtain the most effective results, we too need to identify these things when we pray for healing:

> *. . . and they brought unto him* [Jesus] *all sick people that were taken with **divers diseases** and **torments**, and those which were **possessed with devils**, and those which were **lunatick**, and*

*those that had the **palsy**; and he healed them*
(Matthew 4:24).

Jesus identified some sickness as torment. This kind of torment comes from demonic harassment. It can be mental, emotional, or physical. Mental hospitals and psychiatric clinics are full of people who are tormented mentally and emotionally by demons. These persons have unwittingly allowed Satan room in their thought life with such things as fear, insecurity, hurt, offenses, anger, and unforgiveness. Torments also attack the body . . . Jesus came to heal us of all vexing, tormenting illnesses. With just a word Jesus healed the centurion's servant who was grievously tormented with palsy. Again, He healed a woman's daughter whose sickness was the result of vexing spirits. Jesus was not in the presence of either of the affected persons. You see, Satan has to bow his knee to the Word of God, no matter what the circumstances.

A venerable missionary, one well acquainted with the ways of the devil, tells an interesting account of being tormented by an evil spirit when he was ministering in a foreign land. For a brief period of time, he felt this evil entity trying to attack him through various tormenting things. Then one night his bed just started moving across the floor. Having learned how to deal with the devil, the man commanded, *"Move the bed back, in Jesus' name!"* The missionary said the bed immediately moved back into its previous location.

This same man delivered a young woman jailed for prostitution. While she was imprisoned, terribly painful bites would appear on her body. Both her arms were scarred with the teeth marks of some invisible assailant. Several of the prison officials who tried to deal with the woman died after she put a curse on them. When the missionary read the account in the local paper, God commanded him to go to the prison and deliver the woman. After putting up an argument, he did go and successfully cast the demons out of the woman. She was delivered and healed, accepted Christ and gave up her life of sin, and is still serving the Lord today. What a miraculous "healing"!

The devil comes with a variety of torments for the purpose of afflicting you or making you afraid of him. He will torment you with thoughts, fears, and anxieties, all designed to oppress you and make you his slave. Nagging, persistent things are torments. I put allergies under the category of torments. Allergy-ridden people are continually bothered with headaches, stuffy noses, swollen eyes, and various other symptoms. I think asthma and emphysema are tormenting diseases. Satan's demons come with various kinds of sicknesses, diseases, and infirmities to kill your body; but Jesus came to heal you of all the devil's fiendish torments.

I know a woman who was tormented with allergies all her life. They were becoming more serious all the time; they were sapping her strength and affecting her work. When this person was Spirit filled, she really took hold of healing; and miracle after miracle virtually delivered her family from sickness. However, she was still tormented with the allergies. One day the Lord shocked the lady to attention with a question, "Why do you still have those allergies?" She pondered the question and thought, "Why indeed?" Promptly she applied the healing work of Jesus to the tormenting condition and within 24 hours every symptom was gone. Occasionally the devil tries to bring back a symptom, but she rebukes them and they flee! Sometimes we hang onto tormenting things because we've become so used to them that they just seem a part of us. Don't let the devil torment you that way. Give it back to him in Jesus' name!

The dictionary defines *plague* as "an epidemic disease that causes high mortality." We think of a plague as some dreadful disease that sweeps across a large segment of society bringing with it death and destruction. In the early 1900s a virile strain of flu ravaged our nation. Few homes were untouched, and the death rate was staggering. A plague is also referred to as a continuing or long-lasting illness. Jesus said the woman who had a hemorrhaging condition for many years was sick of a plague.

Polio was a plague that for years put fear in the heart of every parent until a vaccine was found to prevent the paralyzing disease. "Childhood" diseases such as chicken pox and measles can be considered plagues. Scarlet fever and typhoid fever still ravage Third World nations, and recently a plague thought to have been conquered is again raising it's "ugly head." That plague is tuberculosis. Certainly cancer is a plague. It touches large numbers of our population from infancy to old age, and it can attack any area of the body. Modern science has made some strides in helping cancer patients, but this dreaded condition is still a fearsome threat.

There is no question that today we would consider AIDS a plague. In America this hideous, death-dealing disease began in the homosexual community and has now spread to the heterosexual segment of our society. It can also be passed through the filthy needle of a drug user or from blood transfused from an infected person. The statistics of the number who will be infected before the year 2000 are staggering; and if this plague is not stopped, millions of the world's population will die. Medical science is in a "breakneck" race with time to find a cure. BUT—I have good news! Jesus is healing people with AIDS. The name of Jesus is greater than any plague you can name.

In Mark 3:10 we read of Jesus healing many persons who were sick with plagues, and verse 11 infers these plagues were the result of unclean spirits. However, these spirits were no match for the Lord. The people were delivered and made whole. The Lord has never left His people helpless in the face of plagues. When God inspired Moses to write the first five books of the Bible, He said the "blood covenant" people who obeyed His commands would be free from **all manner** of sickness and disease. That includes plagues. Born-again believers are blood covenant people too, and the blood of Jesus Christ will cleanse our blood from any plague.

During the nineteenth century the highly contagious bubonic plague swept across the continent of Africa where John G. Lake worked as a missionary. The British government was attempting to inoculate as many people as it could. Everyone who was known to be ill with the disease was quarantined. Without inoculation, Mr. Lake was going into the quarantined areas to pray for the sick; and many were being healed. However, when the officials heard what the missionary was doing, they insisted he stop. In order to prove that he was immune to the plague, Mr. Lake placed in the palm of his hand some froth from the mouth of a dying patient. Microscopic examination proved the multitude of live germs in the froth died on contact with Mr. Lake's hand. Needless to say, he was allowed to continue his ministry among the sick.

Psalms 91:10 contains a wonderful promise for those who will claim it, *"There shall no evil befall thee, neither shall any plague come nigh thy dwelling."* This psalm contains a treasure of promises and most of them can be applied to healing. Nothing is too hard for the Lord, but we must meet His conditions, *"He that dwelleth in the secret place of the most High shall abide under the shadow of the Almighty"* (Psalms 91:1). To abide under that Shadow is to have victory over sickness and premature death, *"Because thou hast made the LORD, which is my refuge, even the most High, thy habitation"* (Psalms 91:9). When Jesus is Lord of your life, you will *". . . tread upon the lion and adder: the young lion and the dragon shalt thou trample under feet"* (Psalms 91:13). You have power and authority over Satan and all his demons!

When God anointed Jesus with the Holy Spirit and power, He went about doing good, and *healing* all those who were *oppressed* by the devil (see Acts 10:38). I believe oppression begins in the mind when individuals unknowingly accept the "deceiver's" lies. Really, the only thing the devil can use against people is ignorance and deception. If you are ignorant of God's truth about a matter, Satan can deceive you with his lies. The better acquainted you are with the Word of God, the less able Satan is to deceive you. Jesus said, *". . . If ye continue in my word, then are ye my disciples indeed; **And ye shall know the truth**, and the truth shall make you free"* (John 8:31,32).

Unfortunately, many fine Christians have been deceived by denominational doctrine that doesn't agree with the truth of God's Word. How many well-meaning people have you met who are "suffering for Jesus" because they believe this is pleasing to the Lord? These people think their sickness or unfortunate circumstance has been allowed or even planned by God to humble or mature them. They "grin and bear it," but never try to remove it, because they have been told God will reward them according to how patiently they have suffered. This is oppression! No one will ever reach *spiritual* maturity through the affliction of the *flesh*. Such thinking opens the door to whatever the devil may bring your way:

> *Let no one keep defrauding you of your prize by delighting in self-abasement. . . . These are matters which have, to be sure, the appearance of wisdom in self-made religion and self-abasement and severe treatment of the body,* **but are of no value against fleshly indulgence** (Colossians 2:18,23 NAS).

One time a lovely young Christian woman came to me for counseling because she was under very dangerous mental oppression. This lady was attractive, happily married with four young children; the family was healthy, and they were serving the Lord. She had "everything going for her," and yet the enemy had begun to whisper a deadly lie to her. She would be going about her household tasks and this voice would say, "You're going to die. Enjoy life while you can, because you do not have long to live." Assuming the message came from God, she believed it. As you might guess, she soon went into depression.

Fortunately, the insidious lie was exposed when the lady finally shared it with her husband. When he assured her through the Word that God hadn't authored such thoughts, she realized she had listened to the devil. The truth of God's Word set this woman free from an oppression that surely would have taken her life. She rooted up the lies and transplanted Bible promises in her mind and in her heart. She learned that God had a good future planned for her and He would satisfy her with long life. (See Jeremiah 29:11; Psalms 91:16.) She put her thoughts on the Lord, and He brought His peace to her mind (see Isaiah 26:3).

The devil will lie to you and try to make you think it is God. Satan may plant these thoughts directly into your mind, or he may use people to plant thoughts which are contrary to God's will and His Word. In either case if you begin to entertain Satan's lies, they will become vain imaginations and the imaginations will become strongholds. I'm telling you oppression begins in the mind. Once the enemy gets his lies into the arena of the mind, he is able to put oppressive sickness on the body. The devil knows this very well. That is why he attacks your thought life. Oppression is a hideous thing, but Jesus can set you free from any oppression whether it's mental or physical. I'm convinced that mental and physical breakdowns are illnesses of oppression. I would also include anxiety attacks and debilitating stress which causes a variety of illnesses such as spastic colons and ulcers:

> *For though we walk in the flesh, we do not war after the flesh: (For the weapons of our warfare are not carnal, but mighty through God to the pulling down of strong holds;) Casting down imaginations, and every high thing that exalteth itself against the knowledge of God, and bringing into captivity every thought to the obedience of Christ* (II Corinthians 10:3-5).

Notice that the warfare takes place in the mind, but God has given us the authority to cast down devilish imaginations and to bring every thought in submission to the Word of

God. Don't allow Satan to establish strongholds in your mind or put oppression on your body. Cast out every speculation that does not agree with the Word. Use God's Word as the measuring stick for every thought in your mind.

INFIRMITY, BONDAGE, AND CAPTIVITY

Jesus healed people of infirmities. Luke 13:11-13 tells of a woman who had been crippled by a spirit of infirmity for 18 years. Her body was bent over, and she could not stand upright. When Jesus saw this poor cripple, He called her forward and said, *"Woman, thou art loosed from thine infirmity."* Then Jesus laid His hands on her, and immediately the woman stood erect. Matthew 8:16,17 records an occasion when Jesus healed all the sick in His presence:

> *That it might be fulfilled which was spoken by*
> *Esaias the prophet,* [Isaiah 53:4] *saying, Himself*
> *took our infirmities, and bare our sicknesses.*

Luke 5:15 tells of multitudes of people who came to Jesus to be healed of their infirmities. In Luke 7:20-22 Jesus proved to John the Baptist's disciples that He was the Messiah by curing many people of infirmities and plagues.

An infirmity is something that causes a person to be "not firm" or lacking in wholeness. A condition that makes an individual weak or feeble is referred to as an infirmity. Debilitating diseases such as muscular dystrophy or multiple sclerosis can be classified as infirmities. Many wheelchair victims suffer from some sort of infirmity. As some people get older, their bodies lose strength and they become infirm—feeble or tottery. People can become feeble in mind as well as body. Both senility and Alzheimer's disease are infirmities of the mind. The word *infirm* also means "to be unstable or irresolute in one's thinking and actions."

I heard an amusing but very practical story of a woman who applied Romans 8:26 to gain victory over her infirmity—bad eating habits. This scripture says that when we pray in tongues, the Spirit comes to our aid and strengthens us in our infirmities (weaknesses). The lady knew that food was her weakness; so she determined that in her weakness, Jesus would be her strength. Before every meal she prayed ten minutes in the Spirit and found that she was not as hungry as usual. She was able to resist the wrong foods and second helpings. As a result she got down to her desired weight and felt much better about herself, not just in body but in soul. She had won over her infirmity.

I have a beautiful testimony about a grandmother and her five-year-old granddaughter. Ever since the child was two years old, she had been afflicted with a terrible infirmity called juvenile arthritis. The disease had crippled the child until she couldn't walk, so her little body was confined to a wheelchair. The grandmother brought this child to one of my meetings expecting the little girl to be healed. For three days the grandmother had prepared her heart and her mind for a miracle. She had meditated on God's Word and claimed numerous healing scriptures. In her mind she painted a picture of her granddaughter running and playing. This woman purposed in her heart not to leave the meeting until the little girl was healed. That evening during the prayer time, the crippled girl simply got out of the wheelchair and started walking around the room. Jesus healed this precious child of the infirmity. Praise the Lord!

Infirmities or weaknesses are often inherited. We hear of things such as diabetes or heart disease being passed down from generation to generation. When a doctor examines you, he asks if there are inherited diseases in your family. He expects this information to give him clues to your own present physical condition and to aid him in treating you now or in the future. Insurance companies want to know before they insure you whether there are certain illnesses to which you may be susceptible through inheritance. If there are, you are considered a high-risk policyholder.

Although a medical insurer doesn't want to pay a claim for an anticipated illness, the cost of you claiming an inherited infirmity is much greater. Put a stop to such things, and tell these sicknesses and infirmities never to appear again in you or any member of your family. You don't have to have the infirmities of your earthly parents or grandparents; God is your heavenly Father, and He is not infirm! Your inheritance is in Christ Jesus, so don't allow the devil to put any of his infirmities on you:

> *Therefore if any man be in Christ, he is a new creature: old things are **passed away**, behold, all things are become **new*** (II Corinthians 5:17).

One day in the synagogue Jesus read Isaiah 61:1,2 and shocked the listeners by saying the prophet's words were fulfilled in Him that day. (See Luke 4:17-21.) Isaiah said the Messiah would "... *proclaim liberty to the captives, and the opening of the prison to them that are bound.*" Later when Jesus healed the woman who had been bent over for 18 years by an "infirmity," He said she had been *bound* by Satan. This "daughter of Abraham" was in bondage to the devil's evil work, but the Lord loosed her body from the imprisonment which had bound her for so long (see Luke 13:11-16). Jesus said sickness holds people in bondage, but He came to set us free.

Anyone who has been sick knows that sickness is a

bondage. Acute illness puts you in bed, drains you of strength, and keeps you from your regular activities. With less severe illnesses, a person feels like he or she is just dragging around, not able to function normally. The body is bound by sickness. It's as though you have invisible ropes around you that won't let you go. Someone addicted to a habit such as tobacco, alcohol, or drugs knows what a bondage is. These chemicals produce a number of serious, even fatal, conditions in a human body; and most addicts are unable to free themselves from such bondage.

Romans 8:15 contains a wonderful nugget of truth more precious than gold: *"For ye have not received the **spirit of bondage** again to fear; but ye have received the Spirit of adoption, whereby we cry, Abba Father."* Years ago people subjugated other people in the bondage of slavery, but to this day Satan still holds multitudes in the bondage of sin and sickness. However, there is good news; Christ has freed the slaves! All humanity was bound with ''chains'' of sickness, poverty, and death until Jesus bought us out of the slave market of sin with the price of His own precious blood. When we are born again our heavenly Father adopts us into His family where there is life, liberty, health, and wealth.

A woman recently wrote to share this outstanding healing. Her little daughter was hydrocephalic, a condition in which fluid is retained on the brain causing a distorted enlargement of the head. Usually the victim is both mentally and physically handicapped by this atrocious affliction. The mother received a prayer cloth from our ministry; and soon after placing it on her daughter's body, the child's condition began steadily to improve. When the mother wrote to us, her daughter was able to feed herself, comb her hair, and was beginning to speak. What a terrible bondage, but Jesus gave the victory.

We have all heard of Job's suffering, but how many realize the Bible refers to the tragedy and physical affliction that plagued Job as "captivity"? Job 42:10 says, *"And the LORD turned the **captivity** of Job, when he prayed for his friends: also the LORD gave Job twice as much as he had before."*

The story of Job is a perfect example of what Jesus said in John 10:10, *"The thief cometh not, but for to steal, and to kill, and to destroy: I am come that they might have life, and that they might have it more abundantly."* Remembering that Satan was the one who brought the captivity upon Job, we realize that it is the devil who holds us as his captives when he puts sickness upon us. That makes me "fighting mad," and I am determined to free as many people as I can from Satan's prison-house of sickness and disease.

I want to share with you the thrilling testimony of a woman who was healed of multiple sclerosis. She wrote, "I was finally able to let go of all the fears related to the MS which had kept me a *prisoner* for over 24 years. Thanks to God's love and the sacrifice of my precious Lord Jesus, I'm healed—I'm FREE!"

At the age of 16, this lady had been diagnosed with the disease that held her captive for over half her life. Then one day she told a friend she was sick and tired of being sick. Her friend began to open the healing scriptures to her; and after some time, when the woman was convinced Jesus could heal her, the friend's sister prayed for the woman held so long in Satan's prison.

I quote again from her letter, "When my friend's sister laid hands on me and cast out the MS in the name of Jesus,

I felt a warmth all through me. She touched various parts of my afflicted body, and I was a bit scared. Yet I felt a peace and calm when she finished."

The lady saw no immediate improvement, but she kept speaking the Word until she was able to accept her healing as done. From that moment the woman began to improve and today she is totally free from multiple sclerosis, glory to God! This lady wrote to me because during the time after she received prayer and the full manifestation of her healing, she received inspiration through some of my tapes.

SOME THINGS MAY NEED TO BE CHANGED

"Wilt thou be made whole?" This is the question Jesus asked the crippled man beside the pool of Bethesda (see John 5:2-15). Now I ask you the same question: "Do you want to be whole?" Who in the world would not answer in the affirmative? The man to whom the Lord spoke had been trying for *38* years to get into that pool ahead of anyone else, because he believed he'd be healed if he did so. This man's thinking didn't go beyond his crippled body, but Jesus knew the man needed a total healing in his spirit, his soul, **and** his body. Therefore he asked the man if he wanted to be made complete and perfect in his entire being.

Jesus healed the man with just a command, *"Rise, take up thy bed, and walk."* When Jesus encountered the man later in the Temple, He told the man, *"Behold, thou art made* **whole: sin no more, lest a worse thing come unto thee!"** (John 5:14). The emphasis is mine, but I truly believe this is where Jesus put the emphasis. Healing comes from inside out; apparently this man's sinful ways had opened the door to Satan's vicious attack on his body. The Lord warned the man that his attitude and his behavior would determine whether he would stay well. The message of John the Baptist was, *"Repent for the kingdom of God is at hand."* Obviously repentance opened the door for the blessings of God. This meant restoration of every kind including healing.

The Greek word for repent is *metanoeo* which means "to change one's mind and go a different direction." Jesus knows that when people change their minds about sin, He can change the direction of their lives. When attitudes and emotions are changed toward godliness, motives and actions become holy and lives are made whole.

Many times when my mind has not been wholly in line with God's Word, I have not received healing until I've repented and agreed with the truth. When I get my mind in line with the Word, my body gets in line with the Word. Let me tell you of some ideas which can hinder or prevent your physical healing.

Give up the idea that the world owes you happiness. People are so prone to think they deserve whatever it is they want. Folks, the world does not owe you happiness, and there is nothing any of us deserves, outside of Jesus Christ, except judgment. Remember that. There are people who are never satisfied with anything. If they eat in a fine restaurant, they will not enjoy the food; if it's a beautiful day, they remind you that the weather will probably change. If you mention how nice someone looks, these people will find something about that person's appearance they don't like. This kind of negativity is deadly:

> *This know also, that in the last days perilous times shall come. For men shall be lovers of their own selves, . . . lovers of pleasures more than lovers of God* (II Timothy 3:1-4).

In America we have the "gimmies"; our society is geared that way. Advertising is planned to feed the "gimmies" from the cradle to the grave. Of course, you understand the "gimmies"—give me this and give me that. And the more we get, the more we want—and the more discontent we are. However, if we quit demanding for ourselves and start giving to others out of pure, self*less* motives, then we will discover happiness and contentment. When we start counting our blessings and look for the good things in life and in others, we will find satisfaction. *What an environment that is for healing!* I believe our nation can be healed when we, the people, start looking to God instead of self and our own pursuit of happiness.

Give up the idea that you can harbor fear, resentment, bitterness, unforgiveness, anger, and guilt. This is all self-centeredness. Don't think you will continue to enjoy health and healing with this kind of attitude. Thinking like that pours poison into the human system, and negative thoughts are self-destructive. Wrong thinking is sin, and it will demand an awful payment. No one can be warped in their thought life and not become warped in body. Jesus brought salvation to the woman caught in adultery, and said, *"Go and sin no more."* When He healed the man at the pool of Bethesda, He spoke the same message to him, *"Go and sin no more."*

I happened to see a talk-show host interviewing four sisters. The topic was on what to do when you can't forgive someone who has done something "unforgivable." One sister was deeply embittered toward the other because it had been that sister's boyfriend who had murdered their mother. The unforgiving sister blamed the other sister for her mother's death, because she dated a person who was known to be violent. When the one sister had quit dating this man, he had killed their mother to "get even." The other two sisters had forgiven the "offending" one, saying that if she ever needed their love, she needed it now and if their mother were living, she would forgive and try to reconcile her daughters.

Although I don't know whether the counselor was a Christian, he certainly gave godly counsel to the unforgiving sister. He told her she must separate the man who committed the crime from the crime itself. The crime was terrible and wrong, but she needed to forgive both the man and her sister or it would destroy her. He was right on the mark—the young woman was suffering from cancer. What an illustration of how oppression which captivates the mind will also captivate the body! At the end of the show, the audience was told the program had been taped two months earlier. In the meantime the counselor had spent several hours with the four sisters, and the embittered one had come to genuine forgiveness. I like happy endings. I believe the cancer which had laid hold of that young woman will have to release her because she released her sister.

Give up the idea that every healing must be instantaneous. You must exercise your faith for healing at the time you receive prayer, but the manifestation of the healing may come sometime later. Healing may also be gradual, but in either case don't turn loose of your faith. Faith in God's promises will produce the object of your hope. Faith believes for those things which can only be seen in the spirit realm. Your answers eventually will come into view when you continue to believe what you can only see in the Word of God. You do not know all the things God must move into place before healing can happen. For example, I don't believe that the unforgiving sister could be healed of cancer or maintain healing until her mind and attitude had been healed. When Jesus does a work, He desires to do a complete work.

Perhaps healing is manifested sometime after a person receives prayer. However, the more determined a person is to experience healing, the more faith is exercised and the less likely it is that the individual will ever lose the healing. Keep in mind that as far as God is concerned the matter is finished and He is working out the details. Many people come to me days, weeks, and even months after prayer to report their healing. A woman in our church had a growth on her scalp, so she stood for prayer when I was cursing growths, tumors, and warts. She saw absolutely no change in the disturbing growth, but every time her comb accidentally scraped it, she thanked God she was healed. Six months later she reached up to scratch her head and the thing fell off in her hand.

Give up the idea that you can skip spiritual healing and just take physical healing. On a recent trip to Russia, we saw dozens of people miraculously healed. One woman, who had seen many of these healings occur, came to the platform and said, "I see you believe in healing the sick. I'm a 'white' witch and I can teach you some new ways to produce healing." Folks, I don't care if it's a white witch or a witch of any other color, I'm not interested, no matter "witch" way they believe! These people believe they are doing good, but they are tools of the devil. Satan has supernatural power, and he may counterfeit healing; but he is in the business of ensnaring souls, not freeing them. This "white" witch was interested only in people's bodies; but Jesus is interested in the spirit, the soul, and the body. He wants to heal the whole person.

Give up the idea that you can deal with symptoms without getting to the root of an illness. Many times we look at some outward symptom and try to get that healed when there is some underlying problem that needs attention. If there is, the sick person will never enjoy healing and health until the entire issue is brought to light. The Holy Spirit will lead us into all truth; so no matter what the problem, He can show it to us and the appropriate prayer can be prayed. It is so important that we pray effectively in order for the sick to receive not only complete healing, but healing that lasts.

For example, people who have had all kinds of prayer for incessant indigestion and heartburn may not be healed until they change their eating habits. Others with foot problems may have to lose weight, and I've seen people healed in their bodies when they had infected teeth pulled. Not long ago one of our staff members had painful blisters appear on her toes. After she prayed, the Lord showed her the condition wasn't athlete's foot or some horrible dermatitis. All she had to do was remove her nylons before putting on sport socks and tennis shoes when she walked during her lunch period. When she did, the blisters soon disappeared. Even though this person was trying to improve her health through exercise, she was unknowingly scalding her feet.

HOW TO STAY WELL

There are some important keys to staying well. First, anything in your thought life, your attitudes, or your actions that doesn't fit love must *GO*. If you are nursing some hurt or unforgiveness, let them go; if you play unclean fantasies on the screen of your mind, let them go. If you avoid some relative or neighbor because you've been offended, clear the air and let it go. You must walk in love. Not only did

Jesus command us to do so, but a love walk is necessary to stay whole and healthy. The Lord doesn't want unloving thoughts or actions to prevent you from walking in health. Love has correction in it. Loving parents correct their children because they love them, and our heavenly Father corrects His children because He loves them and wants them to enjoy the benefits of health. First Corinthians 13 is a wonderful recipe for love.

The next way to stay in health is to let go of all the crutches. Examine your thinking. Do you sometimes enjoy being sick, or do you believe you have a right to feel the way you do? I heard a minister say that his mother didn't want to be healed of crippling arthritis because she had a right to all the help and attention she received as a result of the condition. She had waited on her children while they were growing up, and she thought it was their turn to wait on her. She had taken care of her husband's needs for years, so she thought it was time he took care of her needs.

You gave up your "rights" when you came to Jesus. You gave up your rights, but you received all of *His* rights. In Christ you have the right to be healed, you have the right to walk in divine health, and you have the right to be whole in every area of your life. Be careful about those crutches that rob you of God's expectations. Don't expect to be sick because you are overworked; don't expect to get the flu when everyone else does. Expect to *be* healed and *stay* healed because that is the will of God. Put God's thoughts in your mind, and remember:

> . . . *if the Spirit of him that raised up Jesus from the dead dwell in you, he that raised up Christ from the dead shall also quicken your mortal bodies by his Spirit that dwelleth in you* (Romans 8:11).

Chapter Nine
GOD'S DINNER BELL IS RINGING

God's supernatural touch in the life of a Christian is His "dinner bell" to the world; it rings out the invitation, "come and dine." Yes, it is a blessing to the one who receives it; but it also affords that person the opportunity to be an undeniable testimony to the unbeliever. The world should see every one of us walking in divine health, divine prosperity, and divine power and authority. It would be impossible for me to count the times I've seen a miraculous healing open the door of someone's heart; and they, too, have stepped into the kingdom to sit and to sup with Jesus and to taste the good things He has for them.

I'm thinking now of a woman who has "sown" a godly life before her unsaved husband. Miracles in her life have repeatedly rung the dinner bell, but the chimes have fallen on deaf ears. Years have gone by, and she has had plenty of time to either give up or keep on sowing precious seeds for an even bigger harvest. Very recently this man was stricken with a serious heart attack. Of course, the devil would like to have taken him out of the game before he reached "home." But how many of you know that God and His team are better at playing the game of life than the devil and his team are at playing the game of death?

This unbelieving husband was touched by the miraculous power of God in such a dramatic way that just a few days after the heart attack, the doctors were scratching their heads in wonder. Every test showed the man has a normal heart as though he had never had a heart attack. Isn't that just like the Lord? In this case, God performed the healing on the unbeliever himself. The heart attack brought the man to attention, and the miracle he experienced in his own body finally caused him to give his attention to the gospel. He can't deny his own healing, and he knows Jesus Christ has a claim on his life. Now the wife has not only seen her husband's physical heart healed, she has seen his spirit touched by the power of God.

The ringing of God's "dinner bell" can be heard all over the earth. God is no respecter of persons; Jesus died for the whole world. God's table is set for every kindred and every tribe, and they are coming by the thousands to His banquet. On one of my last mission trips to Russia, my ministry team and I saw thousands respond to God's dinner bell as we witnessed miracle after miracle of healing. The anointing was so heavy that all the members of the team saw people healed as the team prayed for them.

After one of the meetings, a team member had just stepped outside the building when a Russian lady shoved her daughter in front of her. This lady had "heard" the dinner bell, and she was determined that her deaf child would "hear" it too. Although there was a language barrier, the mother was able to show the woman that her child was deaf. The woman prayed, and instantly the little girl's ears were opened—she could hear! One woman on our team was healed of terrible varicose veins in her legs when three other team members prayed for her. This woman, who spoke fluent Russian, received her miracle at a time when she was "feeding" the Word of God to a group of hungry Russians. Again the dinner bell rang.

God orchestrated another miraculous situation on this trip to Russia. One man and his wife went with gifts and money for a Russian couple they had never met. Friends of theirs had loaded them with the gifts for the Russian couple. The two Russians traveled 900 miles to Moscow, where we were, to receive the gifts from America. The husband and wife were a captive audience in our meeting, and they both accepted Jesus as their Savior and Lord. These precious people received the greatest healing of all, the healing of their souls. I share this story to illustrate how infinitely God cares for all of us. Now this Russian family has the gift of salvation to share with their friends, and the gift just keeps on giving:

Every good gift and every perfect gift is from above, and cometh down from the Father of lights, with whom is no variableness, neither shadow of turning (James 1:17).

Every one of us in Christ has received the power to be like our heavenly Father. Since there is no change in Him, there should be no change in us, except to be continually changing into a more perfect likeness of Jesus:

But we all, with open face beholding as in a glass the glory of the Lord, are changed into the same image from glory to glory, even as by the Spirit of the Lord (II Corinthians 3:18).

When we step on the rung of God's ladder marked "healing," the step we take should be a step up to "health." You'll never progress upward if you take a step backward.

When we have received a healing, it is never God's intention for us to lose it. In the fullness of Christ's humanity, He demonstrated to us that we can continually walk in victory and health through the power of the Holy Spirit. Even though Jesus was tempted in every way we will ever be tempted, His earthly life was continual proof that we, too, can live constantly in the life of God. We don't have to be well today and sick tomorrow. We can be unchanging in the power of God's divine life.

THE UNIQUENESS OF GOD'S HEALING

Look with me at three things that are unique about God's healing power. First, geographical location can't hinder the power of God to heal. When Jesus healed the centurion's servant, the servant wasn't there. Jesus spoke the word and the servant was healed. When Jesus spoke a word in Israel, a woman's daughter was healed in Phoenicia. Psalms 107:20 says God sends His Word to heal. Every time we pray a healing prayer for someone who is not with us, the Word is being sent to heal. I might add that God's power to heal is not stronger in one place than it is in another simply because of location. In America we tend to think everything is better, but I want to tell you more Third World people are being healed today than in the U.S.A.

Next, Jesus always knows the end from the beginning; He knows the outcome of every illness. Jesus didn't rush down to Bethany when He received news of Lazarus' critical illness. He waited in Jerusalem until He knew by the Holy Spirit that Lazarus was no longer ill; he was dead. This was a heartbreaking situation to Mary and Martha, but Jesus knew they soon would be rejoicing over a greater miracle than healing. Jesus raised their brother from the dead. If we stay in God's Word until we are convinced of His promises, we don't have to get rattled and nervous about the end of a difficult matter. We can know that God intends to bring healing and victory every time. That is always His purpose, and He has the power to bring it to pass for those who are trusting in Him.

The third unique thing about the Lord's healing is that

it is complete. He doesn't do a halfway job. However, we sometimes receive healing for one thing in our bodies while another physical problem seems to drag on endlessly. In some cases it seems much easier to believe for the healing of "little" things, while "bigger" things seem beyond the reach of our faith. That is not the way the Lord wants it to be. In His earthly ministry, He made people whole; He didn't leave them partially well or well in one part of their body and sick in another part. Jesus totally cleansed many lepers of their disease, but I know of at least one leper who received a creative miracle. Leprosy eats away parts of the body; but Luke 17:19 tells of one grateful leper returning to thank Jesus, and he was made *whole*.

There is a common notion in "parts" of the Body of Christ that Jesus isn't healing today. Nevertheless, the Lord is still healing multitudes of people all around them. If human bodies were made completely whole by Jesus' touch, I'm certain that God doesn't want some of Christ's Body well and some of His Body sick. It is a tragic irony that there are "parts" of our Lord's Body that remain in sickness because of ignorance and unbelief. The Lord Jesus wants to touch every believer and make them completely well.

Another erroneous notion that persists in the Church today is that the members of the early New Testament Church were never sick because they still had the apostles with them and, for some reason, healing passed away when all of the apostles passed away. That isn't what my Bible says. Not only do I read of occasions when those early saints were sick, I also read Peter's letter which declares our healing was purchased by the stripes (wounds) which Jesus took upon Himself at Calvary. The finished work of Calvary stands forever; and if Jesus is the same yesterday, today, and forever, then you and I are still healed by those stripes!

Paul wrote to Timothy to take a little wine for the sake of his stomach (see I Timothy 5:23). Apparently Timothy had some sort of stomach ailment which was probably caused by the water which often was not too clean in those days. In many parts of the world today, the water is still not fit for drinking. We drink bottled water when we go to Russia; but without thinking, I used some tap water to clean my contact lenses and got an eye infection. Even in the U.S. there are many areas where the people must drink bottled water.

The point I want to make here is that Timothy was sick. Paul could have prayed for Timothy's healing; but if he continued to drink polluted water, he would have continued to be sick. Timothy's stomach condition was probably either caused or aggravated by the water he was drinking. Therefore, Paul recommended an alternative. At another time Paul mentioned that he left Trophimus in Miletum because he was sick. Many people who were healed in the New Testament were not healed by the apostles. Stephen and Philip, who were both deacons, performed great wonders and miracles among the people (see Acts 6:8; 8:6,7). A man in Damascus laid hands on Paul, and he regained his sight. Even Paul who was not one of the original 12 healed numerous people.

AMERICAN PAGANISM

I want to examine some things that are keeping Americans from being healed or that cost us our healing after we have received it. Remember, God not only wants us to *get* it, He wants us to *keep* it! I'm going to deal strictly with those who live in America. Our whole society is being hurt and damaged by wrong thoughts, attitudes, and actions. I call this American paganism. Pagans are irreligious or hedonistic (self-indulgent to the extreme) people. In general, Americans "do their own thing"; if it feels good, we do it—whether or not it hurts anyone else. Praise the Lord, we still have some "salty" Christians who are preserving our nation:

A sound heart is the life of the flesh: . . . Wisdom resteth in the heart of him that hath understanding: but that which is in the midst of fools is made known. Righteousness exalteth a nation: but sin is a reproach to any people (Proverbs 14:30,33,34).

There is the attitude in our culture that you are only young once so live it up BIG. It's the hopeless philosophy of the "eat, drink, and be merry, for tomorrow you die" crowd (see Ecclesiastes 8:15). Our highways have become "slaughter houses" for the drunken driver. Americans spend millions of dollars on "junk" food, and millions of people play on the Lord's day instead of worshiping in His house.

Now, I want to bring this closer to home. Almost without realizing it, we Christians also are permeated with these attitudes. What about the quantities of junk food, carbonated drinks, and empty calories we consume? Or what about the "sipping saints"? Do we think that if it tastes good, we can put it in our bodies without paying the consequences? Christian bodies are not immune to sickness. What about the type of TV and movies we watch, or the books and magazines we read? Let me tell you, folks, if junk goes in, only junk will come out. Let's feast on life and not on death! We will only get one body in which to live this life, and a body used for self-indulgence will surely not be full of health.

Another attitude that has invaded American thought is that we must have instant gratification. We can't wait for anything. We want instant service, instant potatoes, instant coffee, and instant credit. We have "drive up" windows at "fast food" restaurants and banks; we have "fast lanes" at the supermarket and microwave ovens to heat our "prepared" foods. The list of our "modern conveniences" is endless, but we hardly think about it as we sail through life in the "fast lane." Isn't all of this what we deserve?

Let's take a closer look at our "instant" society. Our nation is trillions of dollars in debt, some of our politicians write "bad" checks, banks are "going under," all manner of businesses are going bankrupt, and charge cards have plunged multitudes into incredible debt. And we are slaughtering our unborn future. Where is instant gratification taking us? I know we are not all living this way, and I certainly enjoy my modern conveniences; but the attitude that we must have everything we want at the moment we want it is thoughtless and foolish. It leads to heartache and failure; it leads to sickness and death.

Americans also have a bad habit of blaming some *one* or some *thing* for every problem. We take no personal responsibility for our problems. It is always the fault of someone else. America has a "victim" complex. "I wouldn't be sick if this hadn't happened," or "I wouldn't have these problems if I had been loved as a child." "I grew up in a poor home, my parents were divorced, my teachers didn't understand me." Secular psychology and psychiatry feed these attitudes, but they don't present positive solutions. Some lawyers encourage greedy people to sue for every possible cause—real or imagined—so their clients can get what they "deserve," and the lawyers can line their pockets.

Do you know where all this began? It began with the "fall" in the Garden of Eden. Adam blamed God for giving him Eve, and Eve blamed the serpent; but God held both Adam and Eve accountable for their sin problem. I realize that many people are damaged by the things that have happened to them, and my heart aches for hurting people. However, there is only one way out of the hurt and the pain. People must stop placing blame, accept responsibility for their lives and their future, and give the past to Jesus. He is the Healer—the only One Who can truly heal our minds, our emotions, and our bodies.

Another mark of American paganism is our insistence upon everything being logical to the human mind. We have become so intellectual that if we can't understand something, we won't believe it. Like the old mule, we have to have it all proven to us. When it isn't in the realm of the natural where we can hear it, see it, smell it, feel it, or taste it, we simply refuse to believe. If it isn't explainable, we toss it out. This is ridiculous. If we wait to "figure out" everything, we are going to wait a long time. We are going to miss God, and we are going to miss miracles. Don't miss your miracle of healing because you don't understand how God does it.

How many doctors can explain the essence of life because they know the parts of the human body and how they function? Nevertheless, we still go to doctors. How many astronomers can explain what holds the world in place because they can chart the galaxies? However, the exact precision of the universe is . . . *miraculous*! Can the evolutionist tell you the origin of that first enzyme or slime which he thinks began the process of life? Do theologians understand everything in the Bible? Of course not. Neither do you nor I; but I accept it as truth, enjoy its blessings, and daily expect the Lord to open my spiritual eyes to greater revelation of the truths in His living book.

There is no mortal, no matter what his genius, who can begin to figure out the mind and ways of God. Even the least of God's thoughts are greater than any human thought or imagination, *"Because the foolishness of God is wiser than men; and the weakness of God is stronger than men"* (I Corinthians 1:25). We know that God is never foolish or weak; but with this impossible comparison, we should see that His wisdom and power immeasurably transcend any human thought or strength. In spite of this, the Lord promises to put His wisdom and power to work on our behalf *". . . immeasurably more than all we ask or imagine . . . "* (Ephesians 3:20 NIV).

When we place our trust and confidence in the Lord, He is able to lift us from the natural into the supernatural with one touch of His miraculous power. What difference does it make if we can't understand the operation of God? We can still enjoy all His benefits. The miracle of healing is one of those benefits. God has put into the human body the ability to heal itself, so even without a miracle, your body is a miracle healing machine. Don't abuse it:

> *Let the wicked forsake his way, and the unrighteous man his thoughts: and let him return unto the LORD, and he will have mercy upon him; and to our God, for he will abundantly pardon. For my thoughts are not your thoughts, neither are your ways my ways, saith the LORD. For as the heavens are higher than the earth, so are my ways higher than your ways, and my thoughts than your thoughts* (Isaiah 55:7-9).

If we try to figure out everything, it is going to get us out of faith. I can't explain miracles; but when I need one, all that matters is whether I can receive it. I can't afford to lose faith; that is far worse than "losing face." There is no one who can explain how cancers disappear, discs are replaced in spines, or arms and legs are lengthened. No one can explain how a drug addict or an alcoholic is set free in an instant from those horrible bondages. Nevertheless, anyone who has ever received such a miracle doesn't question that it happened.

Not long ago, I called upon a young man in our congregation to report the healing of his knees. I didn't ask him to tell the congregation how the miracle happened—I just asked him to share his testimony, and we all rejoiced with him. Now he could walk without pain and do many things he couldn't do before. This man didn't know how God healed his knees; he just appreciated and enjoyed the benefits. During this time, I was teaching a series on healing in our church, and we saw miracle after miracle. I can't explain how eyes, ears, and backs were healed; I can't explain how tumors and warts vanished, but they did. Years ago my back was healed when an evangelist prayed for me. One of my arms was longer than the other; but when he prayed, my outstretched arms became the same length before my eyes, and I've never had the back problem since. It was an unexplainable miracle.

DOING WHAT COMES NATURALLY

It is time to look at some of the things that produce sickness in Americans and keep them that way. One of the things is our "supermarket diet"—a diet that is full of prepared food. Nutritionists warn us not to eat the contents of a package if we can't pronounce the ingredients on the label. Much of what we take from the supermarket shelf is either preserved, dyed, or processed. Bugs won't eat this stuff. Why do we? Not even in the produce section are we safe; the fruits and vegetables have been grown in deficient soil and sprayed with pesticide. (See, even the bugs know where to find the good food!) When the produce is picked, it is often dyed or waxed; and then, "to add insult to injury," the grocer puts it under special lights to make it look fresh and wonderful.

As if this isn't bad enough, most Americans insist on eating far too much fat, sugar, and junk food. Look into your neighbor's grocery cart when you are standing in the checkout line. For that matter, look into your own. What do you see? Candy, soda pop, baked goods, chips, dips, TV dinners, and the like. Americans are living off the "fat of the land"; and as a result, we are suffering and dying with high blood pressure, heart disease, cancer, diabetes, and joint problems.

What about exercise—are we burning any of these fat calories? Today most of us sit all day in an office, ride in a car everywhere we go, and come home to eat and sit in front of the TV.

Then there is all the alcohol abuse which is destroying lives. A medical doctor reported that even a few drinks will destroy brain cells. I don't know about you, but I need all the brain cells I have. However, the brain isn't the only thing alcohol destroys; it destroys the liver, the kidneys, the heart. In short, it destroys the body. Liquor destroys on the highway, and it destroys in the home. How tragic that so many people think they can't have a good time or "fit in" with the socially elite without liquor. This liquid drug has captured thousands in the clutches of addiction. I could also mention the devastation that other drugs are causing in our society.

If what Americans eat and drink isn't bad enough, what we do is just as bad. The "sexual revolution" has brought sexually transmitted diseases which are running rampant across our nation. I don't know of any revolution that hasn't claimed lives, do you? The new morality is simply old sin, and the wages of sin is death.

Those of us not sexually promiscuous are not guiltless when it comes to damaging our bodies. We put ourselves under immense stress "keeping up with the Joneses," making our fortunes, pursuing careers, worrying, and whatever else we do to put stress on ourselves. This leads to the next point, which is non-stop work. We are a society of "workaholics"; it's work, work, work, work. While many "burn the candle at both ends," they burn up their bodies as well.

I was thinking about the second generation of Israelites who entered the Promised Land. They were born in the wilderness and couldn't push a cart around a supermarket. Their diet was manna for breakfast, manna for lunch, and manna for dinner. God provided them with very healthy food, and He provided refreshing water that gushed from the rock. Those Israelites also got plenty of exercise. They *walked* everywhere they went; for 40 years they walked—all the way from Egypt to Canaan. When they entered the land of promise, they were "lean and mean," well able for the job ahead of them. Eating right, drinking plenty of water, getting enough rest, and exercise makes any people "lean and mean." However, when you walk down the streets of America today, you don't see the "lean and mean"—you see the fat and lazy.

These are some of the major things we Americans are doing that hurt and damage us physically. We all want to be well, but we also want to do our own thing. People who are sick come for healing prayer, and they receive a miracle. Then they go right out and continue to eat improperly, use alcohol, or mistreat their bodies in some other way and expect to keep their healing. It simply won't work that way. Everyone, without exception, will reap the consequences of his or her lifestyle. When the rules of good health are broken, the Lord is under no obligation to restore or maintain health to the one who abuses the body.

Although it is always God's pleasure to heal people, we see instances in the Bible when God did not heal. Let's examine these occasions and determine why healing was withheld.

Earlier in this book, we looked at the case of Jeroboam's son. Jeroboam knew he was in trouble with the Lord, but he still hoped that the prophet Ahijah would have a good word from God. However, this was not the case and the boy died (see I Kings 14:1-13). There were at least two reasons why the Lord withheld His healing hand. First, He saw something good in the child. God did not want this youngster to grow up in an evil, idolatrous environment and become like his father. God's love spared the child from such a fate. Don't forget that the Lord took the boy to a *far better* eternal existence. Secondly, God did not want any of the seed of sinful, idolatrous Jeroboam to sit on the throne of Israel. What was the cost of the king's sin? It was the life of his only son.

Next, we see the death of King David's son who was born of his adulterous relationship with Bath-sheba. This man cheated and murdered because of his fleshly appetite, but it cost him the life of the little prince. You see, not even kings can break God's rules without paying the consequences. Sin is sin wherever it is found, and it opens the door to satanic attack. David didn't get bitter with God; instead he got better. David found comfort in the knowledge that he would see his innocent son again in paradise, in spite of his father's sin. Because of David's deep repentance, God promised that his next son born of Bath-sheba would sit on the throne. Solomon was that son, and he ruled Israel at the pinnacle of its history.

Lastly, we see Gehazi, the servant of Elisha. This man served his master well until he was tempted by Naaman's riches. After Naaman was healed of leprosy, he wanted to reward Elisha with money and costly apparel. Elisha refused the Syrian general's gift because it was God who healed him. Gehazi, however, just couldn't let this opportunity get away; so he followed Naaman thinking that Elisha would never know. Gehazi lied to Naaman saying that Elisha had changed his mind about the gift, and Naaman gave Gehazi some of the silver and clothing. To Gehazi's dismay, God had shown the prophet what his servant had done. What did Gehazi pay for his "stolen" riches? He paid with his health. The leprosy of Naaman came upon his own body, and the scripture doesn't say that Gehazi repented or that he was ever healed (see II Kings 5).

DOING WHAT COMES SUPERNATURALLY

These are sobering facts. Every action has a corresponding reaction. We cannot sin and abuse our bodies without experiencing the consequences. Just because we feel well and seem to be in good health now doesn't mean we are going to stay that way. If we indulge our appetites, we will pay the price; and it won't just be at the cash register. Before you throw up your hands in despair, I want to give you a recipe you can follow to ensure good health. It isn't impossible—if we commit ourselves to God and a good lifestyle.

The cause of eating right is not hopeless, nor is it cost prohibitive. You will spend more on junk food than you will on nutritious foods. Start reading labels, eat lots of whole grains, fresh fruit, and vegetables. You can buy produce which is actually organically grown. Prepare meals from "scratch," and eliminate as much fat, sugar, and salt from your diet as possible. Reach for the water glass instead of the pop can or the beer can; water is the most healthy, cleansing liquid you can drink.

Don't groan when I mention exercise. Remember, the Bible says that bodily exercise is profitable. Now, it does say that exercise profits only for a little while; but your doctor will tell you the same thing. People can't expect to stay fit if they exercise only once in a while. I don't think any of us eat just once a week or sleep only once a week. Exercise is a vital necessity for good health. Any fitness program should include a reasonable amount of exercise. You don't need expensive equipment; walking is one of the very best exercises there is, and most of us have two legs. In years past people got all the exercise they needed with physical labor, and they walked nearly every place they went.

What about rest? I don't believe it is impossible for the average American to get a sufficient amount of rest. God knows rest is necessary to maintain a healthy body. In every week, the Lord provided one day of rest for His people. Exodus 23:12 says, *"Six days thou shalt do thy work, and on the seventh day thou shalt rest; that thine ox and thine ass may rest, and the son of thy handmaid, and the stranger, may be refreshed."* Jesus told his followers to rest. In Mark 6:31 we read that the Lord called them to a secluded spot so they could rest a while.

In spite of a very busy schedule, I find time to rest. Almost without exception, I am able to nap on a daily basis. If I work later than usual at the office, I have a little hideaway where I can lie down on the divan and nap. When I am flying to an Encounter, I nap on the plane. While teaching an Encounter, I find time during each day to nap. If I'm overseas, I don't forget my nap. I've napped in airports, on planes, trains, and helicopters. I can nap anyplace, even on the floor. Do you think I'm a baby? Well, I've learned that in order to keep the pace I do and stay refreshed and alert to minister to people, rest must be included in my schedule. I don't believe your body is any different than mine.

How do we cope with stress? Stress is an awful thing; and although we may eliminate some things from our schedules, we all have some stress in our lives. Just normal daily routine puts some stress on our bodies and on our minds. If you are a workaholic, examine the things that are driving you to overwork. You must choose those activities in your schedule that have real and meaningful value and eliminate those things that don't. You don't need to be busy all the time to find self-worth. What will you have in the end if you kill yourself with work?

God has an answer for stress too. Daily Bible reading and prayer will put your life into the proper perspective and help relieve stress. There is nothing like time spent with the Lord to put your mind and body at ease. Remember that you have a God who loves you enough to order your days. If you are a Spirit-filled Christian, you have the indwelling Holy Spirit

Who empowers you. He is also with you to guide and comfort you. Learn to rely on Him. The Lord has also given you approximately 7,000 Bible promises to help you through your day. Don't stress yourself with worry and fear; trust God. There is no better recipe for coping with stress.

Now, let's deal with the matter of sex. Americans think they are practicing "safe" sex, but the only safe sex is celibacy before marriage and fidelity in marriage. Any other sex is simply illicit, and the person who practices this type of lifestyle is playing "Russian roulette." The titillating little office affair, or any other affair, will cost the partners more than they bargained. I am so grieved that our teenagers are being taught that it's okay if it's "safe." Today, the "gay" community is anything but gay. Hundreds of them are dying with AIDS, and yet many refuse to admit their perversion is sin. God loves these people, but they have opened their bodies to those things which God warns about.

Some people, who believe in God's miraculous, supernatural power to heal the sick, have the notion that it is wrong to go to a doctor. I don't see that anywhere in the Bible. In Matthew 9:12 Jesus said, " . . . *They that be whole need not a physician, but they that are sick.*" In other words if you are sick, you may need a doctor. The beloved physician Luke was often a companion of Paul's, but I don't find anywhere that Paul rebuked him because of his occupation. There is nothing evil about having periodic checkups or seeing a physician when you are ill. Is a trip to the doctor or taking the medication the physician prescribes going to keep you from being healed if you are trusting God? Go to the doctor and get a diagnosis of your illness; and also see to it that you get prayer for healing. Then you can go back to your doctor with a well body and testify to him of God's healing power.

THE IMPORTANCE OF WORDS

If you were to read the New Testament in Greek you would find two words used to describe God's power. One of these words is *exousia*, and it means "authority" power. The other word is *dunamis*, and it means "miracle-working" power. Dunamis is "dynamite" power. God's Word is the *exousia* or authority of God, and it has great power. When a person believes and appropriates the Word, it can move and change circumstances because the Word is backed by the authority of Almighty God. The One Who framed the universe is the most powerful authority that exists. Every Christian has the authority of God's Word to believe for healing. Without that authority we would have no right to expect healing.

Let me illustrate authority power. I know you all have a healthy respect for that car with the revolving red lights on top. Why is that? It is because the man behind the wheel has the authority to "pull you over" and make life uncomfortable if you have broken some traffic law. The officer wearing the badge doesn't have to outrun you or physically drag you to traffic court. All he needs to do is write a "ticket," and you will appear in court or pay the fine. The officer's vehicle and the badge he wears are symbols of the law which enforces his authority. God's Word is the highest law in the universe, and it is upheld by His authority power.

Now let's look at "dunamis" power. We are all familiar with what a few sticks of dynamite can do to the side of a mountain. Its explosive power will tear away tons of earth. When the first atomic bomb was dropped, the entire world saw the destructive force of splitting the atom. Since then, that awesome power has held the entire world in the grip of fear. However, it was God Who created that atom. Did you know that Hebrews 1:2,3 says Jesus created the universe, and it is Jesus Who holds all things *together* by the Word of His *dunamis* power? The Lord has "dynamite" power ready to be released in miraculous ways for the benefit of all mankind. That miracle power is more than able to save souls, transform lives, and heal physical bodies.

The greatest dimension of God's miracle-working power was unleashed at the moment when life conquered death and Jesus was raised from the dead. Jesus gives that same power to believers when they are baptized with the Holy Spirit (see Acts 1:8). Every time someone is born again, every time someone is healed, God's miracle-working power is demonstrated. However, miracle-working power only operates in conjunction with authority power. If we expect to experience miracles, then we must be in line with God's authority. That authority is His Word.

Jesus always exercised both *exousia* and *dunamis* power when he healed and delivered the sick and demonized. The people marveled at His ability and said, "... *What a word is this! for with authority and power he commandeth the unclean spirits, and they come out*" (Luke 4:36). A Spirit-filled, born-again believer has been given that same ability. We have both the authority of God's Word and the miracle-working power of the Holy Spirit. Don't let the devil "do you in"; overcome him with the Word and the Spirit.

In Luke 10:19 Jesus gave believers authority power to overcome the miraculous power of Satan when He said, *"Behold, I give unto you power* [exousia] *to tread on serpents and scorpions, and over all the power* [dunamis] *of the*

enemy: and nothing shall by any means hurt you."
Although Satan also has supernatural power, he cannot
exercise that power over Christians who know how to use
the Word of God against him. You are able to overcome Satan
by the blood of the Lamb and the Word of your testimony
(see Revelation 12:11). Put the Word of God in your heart
and in your mouth, and Satan must bow to *that* authority.

I have a practical illustration of *exousia* and *dunamis.*
When my children were small, we sometimes left them with
a baby-sitter. With my word I gave the sitter authority to
care for the children while we were gone. However, if Mike
or Sarah did not obey her, I had a stick. That stick was small
but it was mighty. It had amazing "dunamis" power to keep
those two in line. They knew both Wally and I had the
parental authority to use the dynamite of that little stick.

To the religious hypocrites of His day, Jesus said, "... *Ye
do err, not knowing the scriptures, nor the power of God."*
(Matthew 22:29). Even today believers do not understand
the necessity for the Word and the Spirit to work in
agreement. Christians who are baptized with the Holy Spirit
are enthusiastic about the miracle power of God. They
expect to see *dunamis* at work in their lives and in others'
lives, but they are often unwilling to come under the
authority of God's Word in matters such as eating correctly,
resting, etc. Their "pat" answer is, "I'm walking in the
Spirit." These people don't believe God's rules apply to them
because they think the Spirit supersedes the Word. However,
the Word and the Spirit always agree!

On the "other side of the coin" are the fundamentalists
who stand firm on the authority of God's Holy Word. They
claim to believe the Bible from cover to cover; they even
believe the cover. These people will fight to preserve every

comma and period; but when you talk to them about healing they say, "Healing and miracles are not for today." They believe that Jesus authenticated His Person and His ministry with the miraculous, but there is no necessity for miracles today. Therefore, they rob themselves and others of God's miracle power and frustrate the grace of God (see Galatians 2:21). I'm convinced no Christian would willingly sidestep the grace which was purchased for us at Calvary.

Without the authority of the Word and the power of the Spirit working together, believers are out of balance. I want you to think of a bird. Can that bird get off the ground without two wings? Obviously not; nor can the bird sustain flight without the balance and strength of both wings. You, as a Christian, will never soar into the things of God unless you are balanced with the authority of God's Word and the supernatural, miraculous power of the Holy Spirit. Only then can any one of us transcend the natural elements of this world and be elevated into the supernatural life of God.

I want to tell you about a woman who knew both the authority and the power of God. She exercised her faith in both areas and flew beyond the barriers of Satan and sickness into the healing, keeping power of Jesus. In a recent service, the lady shared this testimony. Sometime previously she had had a tumor removed from her back, but evidence of the tumor had reappeared. During the service this lady felt the power of the Holy Spirit all over her, and she knew the tumor was gone. Moments later the Lord showed me that someone in the audience had been healed of a tumor on the back. When I called out this healing, the woman responded. When her husband examined her back, all signs of the tumor were gone—never to return. Praise the Lord!

Christians who are not experiencing healing, or those who

lose their healing may not be living a balanced life. Some may not be accepting the reality of miracles, but others may not be coming under the authority of God's Word. First Corinthians 3:16 declares our bodies to be temples of God. However, multitudes of Christians ignore the warning in verse 17, *"If any man defile the temple of God, him shall God destroy; for the temple of God is holy, which temple ye are."* We wouldn't think of going into our church sanctuaries and defiling them in some way such as eating or spilling food and drink. However, we continually abuse our bodies with improper food and drink, lack of rest and exercise, and other habits which destroy the body.

We must obey God's Word and care for our bodies correctly if we are to experience healing and continue to walk in health. When you were born again, your body became God's temple; and it belongs to Him. When you abuse your body, you are hurting God and preventing Him from continually activating health in your body. Often people excuse their bad habits by saying they just can't quit. Yes, they can. It simply takes submitting our will to God's will. All things are possible to the one who believes. Let's all be bell ringers for God!

Chapter Ten
SIGNS AND WONDERS

Everything looked hopeless; the task seemed impossible. How could it be that at the last minute the mission would be aborted? So many lives were at stake, including the lives of the men in the small boats off the coast of Siberia. However, there was not one man who hadn't known from the beginning how very dangerous this "impossible" mission was. Nevertheless, believing that God is the God of the impossible, they had undertaken the venture with hope and enthusiasm. What an opportunity had been given them to get thousands of New Testaments into the hands of the political prisoners of the Soviet Union.

The small group of men had traveled to Alaska carrying their "contraband" cargo of Bibles, and from Alaska they had flown to the furthermost tip of the Aleutian Islands. There they carefully loaded the precious cargo into the small boats awaiting them; and under a heavy cloud cover, God's "undercover agents" headed for the eastern coast of Siberia. These men and those who helped them had thought of everything including sealing the New Testaments in water-tight containers which would float. Now, they were at the moment upon which all depended; the moment when the Bibles would be thrown into the sea and carried ashore with the ingoing tide.

Somehow, at this crucial point the timing had gone wrong. Instead of a rising tide, the group encountered a receding tide which would carry the Bibles out to sea instead of into the shore. What was to be done? Every minute counted; the men's lives were at stake. If they were spotted, they would be captured. But these Christian men believed in a miracle-working God. In the name of Jesus, they commanded the tide to reverse, threw the Bibles overboard, and as they slipped away unnoticed, they could see the little packages bobbing toward the shore.

Unbelievable, you say? Well, it may be unbelievable to some, impossible to others, but true, nevertheless. This incident took place about 12 years before the collapse of the U.S.S.R., when Christians were being persecuted and it was illegal to take Bibles into the country. We have a big God, don't we? He doesn't want us to believe Him for just the possible things in our lives; He wants us to believe Him for impossible things. It wasn't just men and women of the Bible who received miracles; men and women of faith are still receiving miracles. We serve a living Lord; and because He lives, miracles are here to stay—they are here today!

The Bible begins with a profound, yet simple statement: *"In the beginning God created the heaven and the earth."* This fact is the basis for everything that follows; God is the Author and Creator of all that exists. With supernatural power and genius, the Lord brought into being everything that is natural. What was so in the beginning, still is to the present day; the natural is subject to the supernatural. God controls what He created. This principle is the foundation for miracles! And love is the reason for miracles. God created you and me, and He loves us so much that He will move mountains *or change the ocean tides* on our behalf when we link faith with His "miraculous" ability:

> *Now unto him that is able to do exceeding abundantly above all that we ask or think, according to the power that worketh in us* (Ephesians 3:20).

Miracles are not isolated within the boundaries of "Christian" nations, nor can they be prohibited by hostile governments. Miracle-working faith can be found wherever the Word of God has been preached. I learned of a Russian family who was living on a farm near Chernobyl when the nuclear plant exploded. Radioactive particles contaminated the air, the water, the ground, and the people in a very large surrounding area. Since then the world has seen the horrible results in the bodies of thousands of Russian people. The Russian government actually built a city to house and hospitalize the thousands of people who suffered from the intense radiation. Even children born of affected parents have been born with horrible defects, cancers, and skin problems.

However, this particular Christian family prayed to God for a miracle. These people knew they served a big God Who was much bigger than a nuclear blast—a God Who could protect them when everything around was being permeated with the invisible death. This family prayed and asked the Lord not only to spare them, but to spare their livestock and their land from the contamination. The Lord answered their prayer; and consequently, they were not harmed. Later, when the government examined this family and their animals, they were free from any contamination. Even the ground was clean. What had happened? The Lord Who created the elements had taken control of them.

SUPERNATURAL WORKS BY A SUPERNATURAL GOD

Within the pages of the Bible can be found miracles of every sort and description when God altered the natural course of things by supernatural intervention. We read of the Red Sea opening before Israel and closing over the Egyptians, the Jordan rolling back when Joshua led the

Israelites into the Promised Land, and the bitter waters of Marah becoming sweet when the tree was cast into them. Elisha threw salt into the waters of Jericho and "healed" water which was causing fruit trees to drop their fruit and cattle to miscarry their young. There was the borrowed ax head which he recovered when it came swimming to the surface of the water after he threw a twig into the river. Jesus turned water into wine at a marriage feast. He stilled the stormy waters of Galilee, but later He and Peter walked on that same sea in the midst of a storm.

Whether Jesus stills your storm or walks you through it, He will give you victory. On my first trip to the land of Israel, the Lord took me through a terrible storm over the Atlantic. At this time my husband Wally and I were leading a tour group to the Holy Land. Scarcely out of New York, the plane suddenly plummeted what seemed like thousands of feet. We were flying into a severe storm, and the plane reeled and tossed all the way across the ocean. One woman, who had mustered all her courage to take the flight, was terribly frightened. She prayed frantically for the storm to cease, but the Lord spoke these never-to-be-forgotten words into her heart, "I don't always take you out of the storm, but I will always take you through the storm."

God not only controls the waters which He created; He controls all the elements. Didn't God protect the Israelites from the heat and cold of the wilderness with an enormous cloud during the day and a huge pillar of fire at night? He caused ravens to bring food to Elijah while he hid from Jezebel. There was drought in the land and a meager supply of food, and yet those ravens did not eat the food intended for Elijah. The Lord kept a widow, her son, and that same prophet from starving with a continual supply of oil and meal; and He saved another widow's sons from slavery by miraculously filling borrowed pots with oil. The valuable liquid was sold to pay the family's debts and free the sons.

Over and over we see examples where the Lord miraculously supplied food for the hungry. For 40 years God fed a crowd of two million in the wilderness with manna and gave them water to drink out of a rock. In one instance, Elisha prayed over a pot of soup which had been accidentally poisoned by a wild herb which was added to it. The soup was "healed," and a very hungry crowd of young prophets was able to partake without harm. On at least two occasions, Jesus fed crowds of several thousand with a few loaves and fishes; but God cared enough to provide a miraculous supply of food for just one starving widow.

God cares that much for you. There is not one sickness, not one problem, not one impossibility that God cannot turn into a miracle for you. Even if what you need does not exist, your loving heavenly Father is able to bring it into existence whether it's a new job or a "new" body. Nothing is impossible with our God. Whatever you need, the Lord can supply, even though it may take a miracle. God is able to heal your finances as well as your body. He is able to heal your marriage and change your wayward children. Don't put your confidence in people nor your present circumstances. All that can change in an instant. Put your confidence in God; trust Him. The difference between those who receive their miracle and those who do not is faith. God is not a respecter of persons; He is a respecter of faith.

Not long ago a member of our congregation encountered a demonized man. During the encounter with this crazed person, the man was bitten very badly on his hand. After prayer for the wound, he washed his hurting hand and saw that all the bite marks had "disappeared"—and his hand was as "good as new." I agree that such a thing sounds unbelievable; but if we accept only what we can believe with our natural minds, we will rob ourselves of all the answers which God has for us in His realm of the supernatural. I'm for living a supernatural life where only heaven is the limit, aren't you?

Whatever fiery dart the devil flings at you, God is able to transform the evil into good and make it praise His name. The evil which destroys others need not destroy you. A fiery furnace failed to consume the three Hebrew children who were cast into it, but killed those putting in the fuel. Hungry lions refused to eat Daniel when he was thrown into their den, but these same animals devoured the next crowd before their bodies could even fall to the den's floor. A great fish of the sea swallowed the drowning prophet Jonah and then vomited him onto the coast near Nineveh. The entire city repented of its wickedness when a "water-logged" Jonah preached in its streets, but almost two centuries later that backslidden city was destroyed with a flood. Ironically, Nineveh was saved by water and later destroyed by water.

For the sake of Joshua, God turned defeat into victory when He stopped the sun in its heavenly course and gave His people enough daylight to defeat their enemy. We know that God turned the sun dial back 10 degrees for Hezekiah. God cares as much for His people in this generation as He did for the people of that generation. Although we live in a day when the sun is causing skin cancer and the air we breathe is causing lung disease, the Lord will spare us from all of this when we trust Him to do it. There may be holes in the ozone above us and poisonous earth beneath us, the water may be polluted, but our God is able to deliver us: *"A thousand shall fall at thy side, and ten thousand at thy right hand; but it shall not come nigh thee"* (Psalms 91:7).

Isn't the Lord able to rain gigantic hailstones on His enemies, shake the earth to open prison doors, stop the venom of poisonous snakes, deliver from demons, and rebuke sickness and death? He is not only able, but He has done it before and He can do it again. Don't ever limit the Lord. Believe Him to perform whatever miraculous sign or creative wonder you need. God is unlimited in His authority, unlimited in His power and might, and He is unlimited in His mercy, compassion, and love for you. Always trust Him for the best. When you run out of ideas, He has just begun to think of ways to deliver you!

On one of my first trips to Ethiopia, I was scheduled to fly by helicopter to a refugee camp where the starving people were anxiously waiting for help. I had gone with a large amount of food, and I wanted to get pictures of the camp to use in future endeavors to raise funds to purchase necessities for these precious people caught in the grip of famine and political revolution. When the helicopter arrived, a delegation of U.S. congressmen were given precedence over me and my crew, and there was no room for us. I was not too happy, but I reminded myself that it was the Lord Who had gotten me there for His purpose and He was well able to fulfill that purpose.

So we waited, if not too patiently, for the helicopter to return for our group. When the American men returned, they were all fuming. A constant downpour of rain had prevented them from taking pictures or conducting their anticipated activity. Even though the Americans told us our flight would be useless, we boarded the helicopter, praying and believing the Lord hadn't brought us thousands of miles in vain. By the time we reached the refugee camp, the rain had ceased and we were able to get all the pictures we wanted. What's more, we were able to personally begin the food distribution. You see, God had everything under control for us. My ministry partners had not wasted their money, and I had not wasted my time.

FOUR COMPONENTS TO MIRACULOUS LIVING

Every believer should carefully examine Jesus' ministry for the keys that made Him successful—then use these keys to unlock the door to personal success as a Christian. Does that sound too much like the advice of a "success" seminar? Don't forget that Jesus walked this earth as the Son of *Man*; His resources were no more and no less divine than the resources you have as a child of God. The Holy Spirit was His source of power, and the same Holy Spirit lives and abides in YOU! As a man Jesus consistently followed certain guidelines which not only produced signs and wonders but they also produced a successful life and ministry. Without these things He would never have been able to work the miraculous nor face and endure the agony of Calvary.

We all know that when Jesus walked the earth, miraculous signs and wonders followed Him wherever He went. However, Jesus didn't begin to move in the miraculous until He was baptized with the Holy Spirit. The Lord was about 30 years old, an unknown carpenter from Galilee, when John baptized Him in the Jordan and the Father baptized Him with the Spirit. The Old Testament describes the Messiah as the "anointed one," the One anointed with

God's dimension of power. Not one miracle was ever done in Jesus' own strength; He walked in the power and anointing of the Holy Spirit.

The next crucial thing that I see in Jesus' life is prayer. While the disciples slept, Jesus spent nights communing with His Father in prayer. This two-way communication was the strength of His soul, the direction finder and goal setter for all His time. Returning one noon with lunch, the disciples were astonished at their Master when they found Him already strengthened and satisfied. Jesus explained, " . . . *I have meat to eat that ye know not of*" (John 4:32). Jesus spoke of His prayer life. I believe that morning in prayer, the Father instructed His Son to go through Samaria and stop at Jacob's well. If you recall, while His companions were buying lunch, Messiah introduced Himself to an adulterous woman and led her into the kingdom of God.

Jesus depended not only on the power of the Holy Spirit and time spent with His Father in prayer; He depended on the Word. His every attitude, purpose, and action was wholly in line with the written Word of God. Before we see miracles in Christ's life, we see Him conquer Satan by quoting the Word to him. "It is written," was the guideline for His life; and He continually spoke the Word to all those who listened to Him. The will of the Father was known to Jesus through scriptural revelation. If He had not followed the principles of the Word, He could not have fulfilled its prophecies concerning Himself.

A thankful heart is the next thing of prime importance in Jesus' personal life and public ministry. His whole attitude was one of thanksgiving, and He set this example for everyone around. Jesus kept His priorities right by thanking His Father for the accomplishments of His life. Jesus never looked to Himself; He always looked to the Father and credited Him for the work that was done. Our Lord was in the habit of thanking the Father even before He acted. Do you remember that He thanked the Father before He called Lazarus from the tomb? Thanksgiving marked the simple things in Jesus' life as well as the profound. He thanked the Father before He broke bread with the disciples and before miraculously feeding the multitudes.

There is no question that the Lord also expects His people to be living in the supernatural because He said, " . . . *He that believeth on me, the works that I do shall he do also; and greater works than these shall he do; because I go unto my Father*" (John 14:12). When Jesus went to the Father, He sent back the Holy Spirit to empower believers. As a rule, the people who are seeing and experiencing miracles are the Spirit-filled charismatics of every denomination. These are the "live wires" who spark revival and run everywhere saying, "I can believe for anything"; and they usually do.

Then in John 14:14 Jesus emphasized the next component for living a life accompanied by signs and wonders. He said, *"If ye shall ask any thing in my name, I will do it."* Here Jesus tells us that if we are going to receive God's miraculous answers to meet our needs, then we must spend time in prayer. I think many of us miss God's best because we are not committed to a prayer life. Jesus didn't stop there; His next words in verse 15 include the next component, *"If ye love me, keep my commandments."* The measure of our love for God is measured by our obedience to His Word. A supernatural life is reserved for those who know and love the Word.

For the next component necessary in a victorious, overcoming life, I'm going to quote Paul: *"Rejoice in the Lord alway: and again I say, Rejoice. Be careful for nothing; but in every thing by prayer and supplication with thanksgiving let your requests be made known unto God"* (Philippians 4:4,6). Keep your heart filled with thanksgiving, your mouth filled with the Word and prayer, and your eyes open to the supernatural. Miracles are not something that just "accidentally" happen; they are planned. Live after the pattern of Jesus' life, and signs and wonders will follow you all the days of your life just as routinely as goodness and mercy (see Psalms 23):

And they went forth, and preached every where, the Lord working with them, and confirming the word with signs following . . . (Mark 16:20).

Let's review these four things: baptism with the Holy Spirit, prayer, God's Word, and thanksgiving. The baptism with the Holy Spirit puts a Christian into the dimension of miracle-working power, and it enables the Spirit-baptized believer to receive and to give in a greater dimension. Next, when we put the Word into our prayers, things are going to change because the Word will not return void—the Word will accomplish and prosper God's will. Then when believers get into the spirit of praise and worship, there is no end to the miracles that flow.

This is really a very simple lesson, lived by simple faith. I say faith is simple because faith is simply taking God at His Word. Faith itself is a miracle; and since you can't produce *miracles* in your own strength, you can't produce *faith* in your own strength:

For by grace are ye saved through faith; and that not of yourselves: it is the gift of God: Not of works, lest any man should boast (Ephesians 2:8,9).

Because faith is a gift from God, all you have to do is

receive it. God has packaged the precious gift of faith within the pages of His Word: *"So then faith cometh by hearing, and hearing by the word of God"* (Romans 10:17). Fill yourself with the Word, and you will be filled with faith.

I was so excited by this marvelous testimony sent to us by a retired school teacher that I must share it with you. The woman wrote that she had been diagnosed as having a tumor the size of a golf ball in the upper part of her stomach. The tumor was suspected to be cancerous and supposedly had spread throughout her body. After the lady received this report, she called our prayer line for a partner to agree with her for a miraculous healing. The two of them prayed according to Matthew 18:19, " . . . *That if two of you shall agree on earth as touching any thing that they shall ask, it shall be done for them of my Father which is in heaven."* Together they asked that the tumor shrink to nothing and totally disappear. From that moment the woman continuously spoke healing scriptures to her body and praised the Lord for her healing.

Later, while sitting in the doctor's office waiting for a further examination, one of her hands became intensely hot like coals of fire. She immediately touched the afflicted area of her body with her hand and thanked the Lord for manifesting her healing. When the specialist examined the woman, he found that the tumor had shrunk dramatically, had broken loose from the area where it had been, and was now suspended in her upper intestine by a long stalk. Before the tumor could be removed, it traveled through the intestinal tract to the lower part of the colon. The doctor was able to easily pluck the pea-sized tumor from the woman's body. Today she is totally clear of any sign of cancer, and the specialist said he could take no credit for what God had miraculously done.

MIRACLES THEN AND NOW

In Acts 3 Peter and John went to the Temple at the hour of prayer as was their custom. At the Temple gate, these two Spirit-filled men saw a beggar who had been lame from birth. When Peter caught the man's eye, he said, "... *Silver and gold have I none; but such as I have give I thee: In the name of Jesus Christ of Nazareth rise up and walk.*" Peter took the man by the hand, and at once the man jumped to his feet and began to praise God and leap all around. Peter and John were both baptized with the Holy Spirit; they were men of prayer who prayed according to God's Word and gave glory to God. These men who had signs and wonders in their lives were living like Jesus.

Now I want to look at another miracle in quite a different vein. The account of the sudden and miraculous deaths of Ananias and Sapphira is recorded in Acts 5. You may not view this as a good miracle, but it really is. You see, not everyone was perfect in the early Church any more than everyone is perfect in the Church today. These two people lied to the Holy Spirit, and Peter said they would die for their lie. God had to deal with this sin to keep the ungodly from hurting the infant Church and to show the believers the seriousness of their commitment to Christ. Peter was flowing in the Spirit, and his words were filled with power and followed with miraculous demonstrations.

In Acts 5:12-16 we read that by the hands of the apostles many signs and wonders were wrought among the people. Verse 15 tells us that even the shadow of Peter falling on the sick and infirm had the power to heal: "*Insomuch that they brought forth the sick into the streets, and laid them on beds and couches, that at the least the shadow of Peter passing by might overshadow some of them.*" That sounds as preposterous as people being healed when they received pieces of cloth taken from Paul, doesn't it? Nevertheless, believers accept what they read in the Bible; but many discount unusual miracles today. Let me ask, has the Holy Spirit gone on vacation?

Well, I know He went with me on a trip to China. This trip was very special because our group had taken 16,000 Bibles into that communist country without being detected. It was an extraordinary feat, so we were all "high" in the Spirit. However, the miracles were not over. One day our group was headed for the "Great Wall" when a lady in our group pointed her finger at the bus window and shouted, "In the name of Jesus, arise and walk." Then I saw the bent and crippled man standing in the shadow of the bus. Although the cripple neither saw nor heard the lady, he suddenly stood erect and burst out laughing. He was ecstatic over his "mysterious" healing; and after the bus passed, we could still see him doing a little "jig" on the street corner. I would have to say that signs and wonders have not diminished through the ages. Didn't Jesus say we would do greater works than He?

The Holy Spirit even travels to Russia with us on our tours. One afternoon in Kiev the group had gone to see a beautiful, old monastery. Just as we emerged from the building and stepped back onto the street, we saw two women sitting on a little bench. One of the women seemed quite feeble, and she was holding tightly to a cane. Moved with compassion, a Spirit-filled psychologist who was with us said, "In Jesus' name, get up and walk." She was close enough to cast her shadow on the two women; but the dear Russian lady had no idea that the American was speaking to her, and she certainly didn't know what the psychologist said. However, there are no language barriers to the Holy Spirit. The feeble little lady suddenly stood up, dropped her cane, and walked off. Her startled friend hurried up the street to catch her companion.

In Acts 8 the Holy Spirit led Philip the deacon to Samaria. We might think those awful Samaritans didn't deserve miracles. The Jews hated them because they were a "mongrel bunch" who were involved in idolatry and sorcery. Nevertheless, it was in this place where the Holy Spirit poured out a mighty revival which was accompanied by many amazing signs and wonders. Simon the sorcerer was saved, and multitudes of the people were saved and healed. When Peter and John joined Philip, they prayed and the entire group received the baptism with the Holy Spirit.

It is obvious that Satanism and sorcery didn't pass away with the revival in Samaria. What would have horrified all of us a decade or two ago is almost commonplace in today's society. Young people, looking for meaning in their lives, are being sucked into these devilish practices; and even professional people are practicing satanists because they have found a source of power. However, the power of God is still greater than any of Satan's power; and when these deluded individuals see the power of God at work, they willingly turn their lives over to Christ and receive His mighty power. I personally know two men who were satanic priests, but now they are ministering for the Lord Jesus Christ. We are continually seeing people set free from the devil's deceptions.

In Acts 16 we find two Spirit-filled men praising and worshiping God. That doesn't sound too unusual, does it? Spirit-filled believers are always praising the Lord. However, these were unusual circumstances. These two men have just had their backs ripped open with a scourge, they have been placed in irons in the deepest dungeon of a Philippian jail, and it's midnight! What's more, these two are innocent men. Even the most "turned on" Christian might find this a time to moan and groan—just a little. And yet, in the midst of their difficulties, Paul and Silas sang praises to the Lord because they *knew* their God.

Paul and Silas weren't necessarily looking for a miracle, but they were open to one—and so were the gates of the prison. Suddenly the earth shook and those prison doors opened. It is a miracle the entire prison didn't collapse on Paul and Silas; but God knew what He was doing, and the two prisoners followed His leading. Instead of fleeing, Paul and Silas took advantage of the miraculous circumstance. The frightened jailer took them home with him to dress their wounds; and while there, the "captives" led their captor and his family to Jesus. The jailer discovered he was the one who was the prisoner—a prisoner of sin, but he and the members of his family were set free.

Did you know that God can shake a home, open doors, and set prisoners free today? Here's a quote from a praise report recently written to our ministry: "I have been re-united with my husband after 23 years. We have both changed for the better, and we still love each other." The woman explained that she had finally placed the whole matter on the altar, and called our prayer line to ask for the reconciliation of her entire family. She said she had no idea that her husband would return or that God could possibly straighten out their financial situation, which she said was "in a mess." Nevertheless, even as she was writing the letter, she received a call informing her of a large settlement of money which further untangled "the mess."

Within recent months the homes of two pastors I know have burned to the ground. Without a doubt, Satan intended to destroy these men, their families, and, consequently, their ministries. However, every member of each family was miraculously saved; and what Satan intended for evil has been turned to good. Both of these men have an even greater zeal for the Lord, and a *fire* in their ministry. One of these homes was older and in need of some repair. Now the couple and their children will soon be moving into a beautiful new home. Ha, ha, devil!

When Paul was miraculously converted on the road to Damascus, Satan lost one of his "best" sinners and Jesus won a saint who evangelized most of the civilized world and wrote most of the New Testament. Signs and wonders accompanied Paul wherever he went. On one occasion Paul was stoned and dragged out of the city of Lystra. When the believers gathered around Paul and prayed, he stood to his feet. The next day he walked about 20 miles to the city of Derbe. Personally, I believe that Paul was raised from the dead; but whether he was dead or not, Paul certainly received a miraculous healing. In those days the people didn't stop until a body was completely covered with a pile of boulders. Just one heavy rock would crush a skull or break a bone.

There's an almost amusing story in Acts 20:7-10. Paul was preaching to a group of people in the city of Troas, and he was very "long-winded." As a matter of fact, Paul preached until midnight; and a very tired young man named Eutychus fell asleep. Now that wouldn't be too tragic; some people today go to sleep in church. But this fellow was sitting on the window ledge of the third-story room where the meeting was held. Instead of tumbling to the inside, Eutychus fell three floors to the ground below—and died. Paul simply went down and raised him from the dead. Then the happy congregation continued the meeting until daybreak.

The book of Acts is a book of signs and wonders. It is full of miracles from the first page to the last page, but did you know that Acts is the only book of the Bible that really has no ending? Why is that, you ask? The book of Acts is a record of the acts of the Holy Spirit, and He hasn't stopped acting yet in the lives of people. Time doesn't stop Him; "Iron Curtains" and "Bamboo Curtains" don't stop Him. Walls don't stop Him, governments don't stop him, "impossible" situations don't stop Him, incurable diseases don't stop Him, and neither does the unbelief of some stop Him. The Holy Spirit is on the move, and I'm sure you want to move with Him. Let's all get under the spout where the glory comes out!

Just the other day a lady on our staff was watching a Christian television program. One of the guests on the program was a Spirit-filled Catholic priest who works among the poor in the towns on both sides of the U.S.-Mexican border. This priest reported the supernatural multiplication of food, miraculous healings, and he even told of a woman being raised from the dead after the doctor had written the death certificate. Several young, mentally retarded children who lived on a dump were completely healed. Their retardation was due to protein deficiency in their diets when they were babies, and they couldn't learn. However, after a compassionate teacher prayed for the children, their minds became perfectly normal.

People have a tendency to relegate signs and wonders to the dusty archives of Biblical history or to the "big name" evangelists. However, there are no big names in the work of the ministry. There never were and there aren't now. The only big name is Jesus! It was in that name that Peter, Paul, James, and John prayed. Philip used that name to work miracles, and the Bible doesn't even mention the names of many who performed miracles in the only name that has miraculous power. None of these people ever considered themselves to have a "big name."

The Lord took an arrogant, demanding Saul, transformed him, and renamed him Paul. Saul means "demanding"; and as Saul, this man, who saw himself as very big and important, was an enemy of Christ and His Church. Paul means "small," which is exactly how Paul saw himself after his miraculous encounter with the One Whom he persecuted. Nevertheless, Paul was able to say in the face of every circumstance, " . . . *when I am weak, then am I strong*" (II Corinthians 12:10). This man proved with many signs and wonders that human weakness is superimposed by the strength of Jesus when a person stays small enough to be hidden in Christ.

Jesus gave every believer—from the past right up to this present hour—the power of attorney to use His name. You, too, can work the miraculous in the power of that name. Signs and wonders of every sort and description ought to follow you. Don't wait for some "big name" to come along; the name of Jesus has been entrusted to you.

The power in that name will heal bodies, it will heal minds, it will heal marriages, it will heal homes, it will heal finances. It will heal any circumstance. By the power vested in the name of Jesus anything that needs healing can be healed. My challenge to you is "be healed" and go take healing to others in His precious name.

Visit
Marilyn Hickey Ministries'
Website

www.mhmin.org

Receive Jesus Christ as Lord and Savior of Your Life.

The Bible says, *"That if thou shalt confess with thy mouth the Lord Jesus, and shalt believe in thine heart that God raised him from the dead, thou shalt be saved. For with the heart man believeth unto righteousness; and with the mouth confession is made unto salvation"* (Romans 10:9,10).

To receive Jesus Christ as Lord and Savior of your life, sincerely pray this prayer from your heart:

Dear Jesus,

I believe that You died for me and that You rose again on the third day. I confess to You that I am a sinner and that I need Your love and forgiveness. Come into my life, forgive my sins, and give me eternal life. I confess You now as my Lord. Thank You for my salvation!

Signed _____ Date _____

Please print.

NAME Mr. & Mrs.
      Miss
      Mr.
      Mrs. _____

ADDRESS _____

CITY _____

STATE/PROVINCE _____ ZIP/POSTAL CODE _____

COUNTRY _____

PHONE (H) (   ) _____ (W) (   ) _____

EMAIL _____
Please include your email address so you can receive periodic updates.

Write or call...

We will send you information to help you with your new life in Christ:
• Marilyn Hickey Ministries • P.O. Box 17340 • Denver, CO 80217
For prayer call TOLL-FREE (U.S. only): 1-877-661-1249.
For product orders call: 1-888-637-4545.

On the World Wide Web at: www.mhmin.org

For Your Information
Free Quarterly Magazine

☐ Please send me your free
quarterly magazine, OUTPOURING.

Tapes and Books

☐ Please send me Marilyn and Sarah's latest product catalog.

Mr. & Mrs.
Mr.   Please print.
Miss
Name Mrs. _____

Address _____

City _____

State/Province _____

Zip/Postal Code _____

Country _____

Phone (H)   (   ) _____

         (W)   (   ) _____

Email_____
Please include your email address so you can receive periodic updates.

Mail: Marilyn Hickey Ministries
           P.O. Box 17340 • Denver, CO 80217

Call: 1-888-637-4545 TOLL-FREE, U.S. only,
           weekdays, 6:30 a.m.—4:30 p.m. (MT)

Logon: www.mhmin.org

BOOKS BY MARILYN HICKEY

Angels All Around $7.95

Be Healed $9.95

Breaking Free From Fear $4.99

Breaking Generational Curses $16.99

Building Blocks for Better Families $4.95

Devils, Demons, and Deliverance $9.95

Freedom From Bondages $7.95

God's Covenant for Your Family (English or Spanish) $7.95

He Will Give You Another Helper $14.95

How to Be a Mature Christian $7.95

Know Your Ministry $4.95

Names of God (The) $7.95

Maximize Your Day . . . God's Way $7.95

Wow Faith $12.99

Satan-Proof Your Home $7.95

Soul Food Daily Nourishment from Psalm 119 .... $11.95

What Every Person Wants to Know About Prayer $4.95

You Can! Bounce Back From Your Setback $19.95

Your Miracle Source $4.99

Your Total Health Handbook—Body • Soul • Spirit $9.95

By Sarah Bowling

Fearless on the Edge: Knowing What To Do With Every Challenge $4.95

Revival of the Bible $12.99

The 9 Secrets of Spiritually Successful People $7.95

Solutions: Grace Applications for your Everyday Situations $4.95

To order call TOLL-FREE (U.S. only), weekdays,
6:30 a.m. to 4:30 p.m. (MT), at 1-888-637-4545
or to order online go to www.mhmin.org.

Get Your Miracle!

Marilyn Hickey
PRAYER CENTER

CONTACT the Prayer Center...prayer warriors will pray God's Word and apply the power of the "prayer of agreement" to your needs. *"...If two of you agree on earth concerning anything that they ask, it will be done for them by My Father in heaven"* (Matt. 18:19 NKJ). Then see the results!

Call: 1-877-661-1249
TOLL-FREE, U.S. only, weekdays,
6:30 a.m.—6:00 p.m. (MT)

Fax: 1-303-770-2752
(U.S. & International Prayer Requests)

Need Prayer Now?

Logon: www.mhmin.org

Marilyn Hickey Ministries

Marilyn was a public school teacher when she met Wallace Hickey. After their marriage, Wally was called to the ministry and Marilyn began teaching home Bible studies.

Marilyn and Wally adopted their son Michael. Then through a fulfilled prophecy they had their daughter Sarah who, with her husband Reece Bowling, is now part of the ministry.

The vision of Marilyn Hickey Ministries is to "cover the earth with the Word"(Isaiah 11:9). For more than 30 years, Marilyn Hickey has dedicated herself to an anointed, unique, and distinguished ministry of reaching out to people—from all walks of life—who are hungry for God's Word and all that He has for them. Millions have witnessed and acclaimed the positive, personal impact she brings through fresh revelation knowledge that God has given her through His Word.

Marilyn has been the invited guest of government leaders and heads of state from many nations of the world. She is considered by many to be one of today's greatest ambassadors of God's Good News to this dark and hurting generation. The more Marilyn follows God's will for her life, the more God uses her to bring refreshing, renewal, and revival to the Body of Christ throughout the world. As His obedient servant, Marilyn desires to follow Him all the days of her life.

Marilyn founded her ministry "Life for Laymen" so that she could reach more people with her gift for practical Bible application.

Marilyn taught at Denver's "Happy Church"—now Orchard Road Christian Center (ORCC)—and hosted ministry conferences with husband Wally, pastor of ORCC.

At a retreat in 1976, Marilyn realized she was called to "cover the earth with the Word."

The ministry staff in the early days helped Marilyn answer the mail that came in response to her first 15-minute radio show.

Soon Marilyn realized she could reach more people through television. She and Wally hosted many well-known guests.

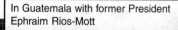
In Guatemala with former President Ephraim Rios-Mott

Marilyn has been the invited guest of government leaders and heads of state from many nations of the world.

In Egypt with Mrs. Anwar Sadat

In Venezuela with former first lady Mrs. Perez

Marilyn ministered to guerillas in Honduras and brought food and clothing to the wives and children who were encamped with their husbands.

The popular Bible reading plan *Time With Him* began in 1978 and invited people to "read through the Bible with Marilyn." The monthly ministry magazine has since been renamed *Outpouring*. It now includes a calendar of ministry events, timely articles, and featured product offers.

Through Word to the World College (formerly Marilyn Hickey Bible College), Marilyn is helping to equip men and women to take the gospel around the world.

Sarah Bowling taught at Riverview Christian Academy for several years before her marriage, wrote correspondence courses for the Bible college...and has since joined the ministry full-time where she combines speaking engagements and teaching at WWC with ministry trips and Crusades.

God opened doors for the supplying of Bibles to many foreign lands—China, Israel, Poland, Ethiopia, Russia, Romania, and the Ukraine, just to name a few.

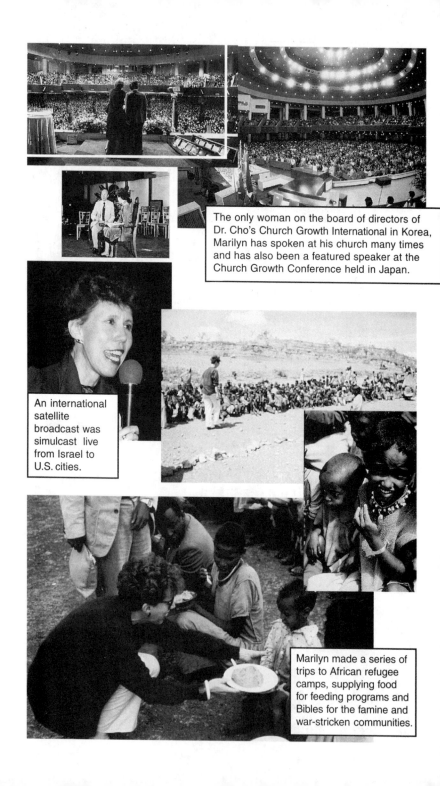

The only woman on the board of directors of Dr. Cho's Church Growth International in Korea, Marilyn has spoken at his church many times and has also been a featured speaker at the Church Growth Conference held in Japan.

An international satellite broadcast was simulcast live from Israel to U.S. cities.

Marilyn made a series of trips to African refugee camps, supplying food for feeding programs and Bibles for the famine and war-stricken communities.

Sarah began traveling overseas with her parents at an early age and developed a heart for missions.

Both Marilyn and Sarah have a strong heart for China, and have distributed thousands of Bibles and tracts there and in Russia.

The ministry expanded from its beginnings in a cardboard box of files on a kitchen table, to the first International Ministry Center, built in 1985, to its present headquarters located in Greenwood Village, Colorado.

FILL THE SHIP, a special project of the Marilyn Hickey Children's Fund, supplies food and Bibles to various Third World countries, such as Haiti, the Philippines, Ethiopia, Honduras, and El Salvador.

The prime time television special, "A Cry for Miracles," featured co-host Gavin MacLeod.

Marilyn has been a guest several times on the 700 Club with host Pat Robertson.

Marilyn ministered in underground churches in Romania before the European communist countries were officially open.

Marilyn Hickey's Prayer Center handles calls from all over the U.S.— ministering to those who need agreement in prayer.

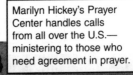

More than 1,500 ministry products help people in all areas of their life.

Marilyn received her honorary doctorate from Oral Roberts University. She now serves as the chairman of the Board of Regents.

Sarah graduated from ORU, and later earned her Master's in History.

Marilyn and her Faith Covenant Partners respond to countless needs across the world. . .the devastating earthquakes in Mexico City, Romanian orphans, leprosy victims in Africa, orphans in war-torn Rwanda, street children in Brazil. . . all are touched by God's power.

MHM supports Mission of Mercy in Calcutta, headed by Huldah Buntain. Marilyn has made several trips there.

Airlift Manila provided much needed food, Bibles, and personal supplies to the Philippines; MHM also raised funds to aid in the digging of water wells for those without clean drinking water.

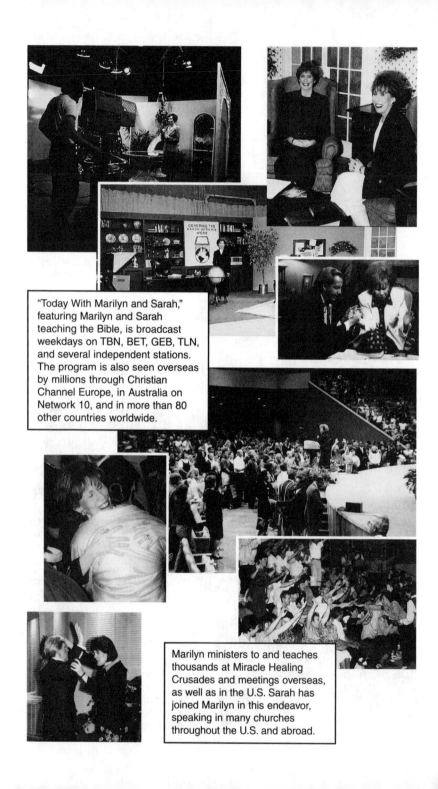

"Today With Marilyn and Sarah," featuring Marilyn and Sarah teaching the Bible, is broadcast weekdays on TBN, BET, GEB, TLN, and several independent stations. The program is also seen overseas by millions through Christian Channel Europe, in Australia on Network 10, and in more than 80 other countries worldwide.

Marilyn ministers to and teaches thousands at Miracle Healing Crusades and meetings overseas, as well as in the U.S. Sarah has joined Marilyn in this endeavor, speaking in many churches throughout the U.S. and abroad.

Exciting ministry opportunities awaited Marilyn, Sarah, and their team of travelers in the Ukraine and Russia, as the doors opened for the Gospel.

Victim of the nuclear power plant disaster in Chernobyl

Marilyn has held Bible Encounters in Malaysia and Singapore, and ministered to Vietnamese in a refugee camp.

National Womens' Conferences and Pastors' Wives' Conventions were held across the U.S., exhorting women to "Change Their World!"

"Mastering Your Ministry: A Woman's Mentoring Clinic" is Marilyn's new concept for providing in-depth teaching and personal ministry in an intimate setting.

The New York area Crusade hosted well-known ministers and ministered to thousands at the Meadowlands Arena in New Jersey.

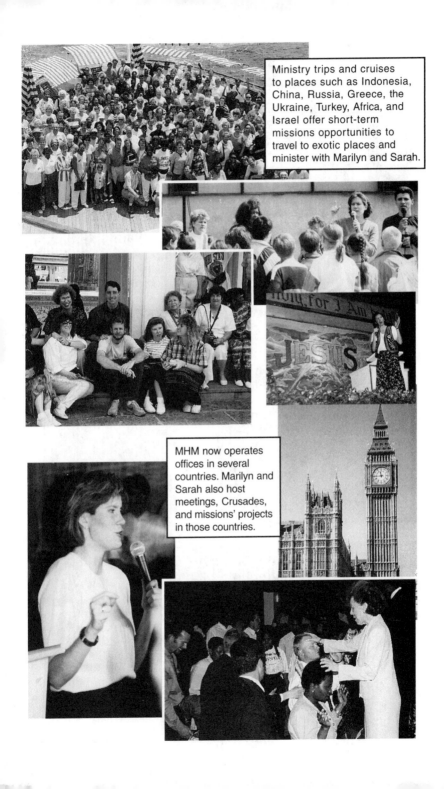

Ministry trips and cruises to places such as Indonesia, China, Russia, Greece, the Ukraine, Turkey, Africa, and Israel offer short-term missions opportunities to travel to exotic places and minister with Marilyn and Sarah.

MHM now operates offices in several countries. Marilyn and Sarah also host meetings, Crusades, and missions' projects in those countries.

Crowds of up to 200,000 attended the open-air Crusade in Bangalore, India.

In Islamabad, Pakistan, Marilyn held a Ministry Training School. Total Crusade attendance was estimated at 70,000.

Ministry Training Schools are held in many Third World countries, such as Sudan and Tanzania, and provide training and native language literature for local pastors and church leaders. Nightly Crusades are held to minister to the local populations.